ANOINTED TO REIGN II

Dr. Ronald E. Cottle

Christian Life Educators Network (CLEN) is a world-wide network of member schools in affiliation with CLST Global. CLEN offers complete support services to member schools and students. Through an articulation agreement with CLST Global, students in CLEN schools can earn CLST Global Certificates, Diplomas and Degrees.

Christian Life School of Theology Global (CLST Global) has met the requirements for exemption from applicable Georgia law as a religious institution under the provision of the Post-secondary Educational Authorization Act, Georgia Code 20-3-100 et seq. As a result, CLST Global awards a variety of Ministry Certificates, Diplomas and Degrees ranging from an Associate of Theology through a Doctor of Sacred Studies.

CHAPTER ONE

WHEN YOU OFFER YOUR BEST AND GOD SAYS "NO"

> *And it came to pass, when the king sat in his house, and the LORD had given him rest round about from all his enemies*
>
> *That the king said unto Nathan the prophet, See now, I dwell in an house of cedar, but the ark of God dwelleth within curtains.*
>
> *And Nathan said to the king, Go, do all that is in thine heart; for the LORD is with thee.*
>
> *And it came to pass that night, that the word of the LORD came unto Nathan, saying,*
>
> *Go and tell my servant David, Thus saith the LORD, Shalt thou build me an house for me to dwell in?*
>
> 2 Samuel 7:1–5

It was a great idea—something that had *never been done before*. The aches and pains of the most recent campaign had healed long ago, and this season the warrior king finally had time to enjoy the calming cedar fragrance of his new royal residence. He suddenly felt uncomfortable again, and then the idea exploded in his mind.

Here I sit in my brand new home, resting and feasting in the goodness of God . . . yet He still visits with us under an embarrassing tent as if He is less than a mere vagabond wanderer of the desert. Someone has to do something about it—surely He has blessed me for just this purpose!

It was a shocking proposal. No one had ever dared to attempt such a thing! The idea was so original and the purpose so grand that King David (representing the apostolic anointing of the church era) felt led to share it and verify it with the trusted prophet and seer, Nathan. This was a very wise move by David.

The idea seemed utterly selfless on the surface. It would glorify the God of Israel, and it might even draw most of the people in the freshly unified kingdom of Israel and Judah into more intimate and personal knowledge of their invisible God. It made sense. It felt good.

But evidently, it wasn't good enough.

After decades of virtually non-stop war under its first two kings, Israel finally was enjoying some good times.

At what seemed to be the high point of the legendary King David's reign, the "sweet psalmist of Israel" experienced what you may be experiencing right now in your life.

David made what he believed to be "the ultimate commitment" to his Lord. He wanted to build God a "house" in which to dwell, but his dream burst in a single paragraph.

> But God said unto me, *Thou shalt not* build an house for my name, because thou hast been a man of war, and hast shed blood (1 Chronicles 28:3, emphasis mine).

David received God's "no" within twelve hours, but it may have taken him years to discover and accept the reason his ultimate commitment was transformed into his son's lifetime achievement. Perhaps you, too, have offered God the best you have!

Did you offer to serve Him in places few others would dare to go?

Perhaps you said, "Lord, I'll go to India . . . China . . . Africa . . ."?

Were you one of the few to say to the Lord of the Harvest, "I'll minister to the homeless . . . to drug addicts . . . to HIV/AIDS victims and their families"?

You offered Him your best, your all. Yet, in spite of your sincerity, submission and sacrifice, *does it seem as if God said "No"*?

Understand this: **God never wastes a wound, a failure, or a learning moment in your life.** As He declared through the prophet Jeremiah:

> For I know the thoughts that I think

toward you, says the LORD, thoughts of peace and not of evil, to give you a future and a hope (Jeremiah 29:11, NKJV).

Everything in God's dealings with and through you proceed from the plans He made for you even before your birth. Understand that God *never* "does nothing." He is always at work doing something in and through you—even when it feels or appears to be otherwise. For this reason and more, sometimes a *no* from God can do more than a divine *yes*.

God often uses His NO to:
- ## Take you FARTHER
- ## Make you BETTER
- ## Use you in GREATER WAYS

In other words, the God who "declares the end from the beginning" (see Isaiah 46:10) *accomplishes just as much through His DENIALS in your life as He does through His PERMISSIONS!*

How can this be? To understand this powerful principle of success, let us consider three things:

1. *When* God says *no*.

2. *What to do* when God says *no*.

3. What God *is really saying* when He says *no*.

When God Says "No"

When God said *no* to David, Israel's shepherd-king *was at a good place in his life* according to at least five major circumstances or events recorded in God's Word.

First, David's kingdom was finally established and he realized it. In 2 Samuel 5:12, we read, "And David perceived that the LORD had *established* him king over Israel, and that he had exalted his kingdom for his people Israel's sake." The Hebrew word translated "established" in this verse means "to bring into incontrovertible existence." David was planted incontrovertibly into divine purpose as king of Israel, and no one could do anything about it.

The New Covenant equivalent of being "established in purpose" appears in Romans 8:28, which says, "And we know that all things work together for good to them that love God, to them who are the called according to his purpose." Because the word "his" does not appear in the original Greek, Paul is perfectly mirroring the Old Covenant understanding when he speaks of us being "*called according to purpose.*" There is only one true purpose in the earth, the original purpose of the Creator.

Second, David's enemies were subdued, and in a supernatural manner. Almost immediately after David was crowned king over a newly reunified Jewish nation, his most determined enemies showed up ready for revenge.

> Once more the Philistines came up and spread out in the Valley of Rephaim; so

5

> David inquired of the LORD, and he answered, "Do not go straight up, but circle around behind them and attack them in front of the balsam trees. As soon as you hear the sound of marching in the tops of the balsam trees, move quickly, because that will mean the LORD has gone out in front of you to strike the Philistine army." So David did as the LORD commanded him, and he struck down the Philistines all the way from Gibeon to Gezer (Samuel 5:22–25, NIV).

Third, as a first order of business, the Ark of God—long held in hostile Philistine hands—was finally returned and set in Zion under David's rule. We read in 2 Samuel 6:17, "And they brought in the ark of the LORD, and set it in his place, in the midst of the tabernacle that David had pitched for it: and David offered burnt offerings and peace offerings before the LORD."

Fourth, David was living in his dream house, a royal palace far different from an outlaw's cave or the rugged surroundings of a shepherd's wilderness shelter. This house was a designer's dream, a royal treasure custom-built on a grand scale.

> And Hiram king of Tyre sent messengers to David, and cedar trees, and carpenters, and masons: and they built David a house (2 Samuel 5:11).

Fifth, David was finally "at peace" because ". . .

the LORD had given him rest round about from all his enemies" (2 Samuel 7:1).

"God, I Really Want to . . ."

Just when everything seemed to be so right, David shared the missing piece, the *greatest desire of his heart*, with his friend and prophetic confidante, Nathan. I can almost hear King David as he leans close to the prophet and says:

> "Nathan, do you know what I *really* want to do? I'm thankful for the victory over Goliath and the Philistines, and I'm really glad that we made it through the tough years with King Saul hunting for us. But what I really *want* to do is to *build God a house.* I know it sounds strange, but He has given me everything. It's time for me to give Him something He's never had before. What do you say?"

Apparently this was the first time David publicly expressed his deepest passion, but from this point it remained a central focus of his life. He had already accomplished much, but he wanted to do something more.

Anyone who is truly saved, called and anointed will feel an inner urge to "do something more." If this urge is pursued, he will develop a great resolve to count or amount to something for the Kingdom of God. Believers who really love God

want to do something with their lives to glorify
God.

On the other hand, we all know people who
were saved, called and blessed. Some even
achieved their "house of cedars," but somehow
along the way they forgot their early consecration.

This was *not* David's problem. His passion for
God burned brightly, so he spoke to Nathan the
prophet seeking God's will in the matter. The
weight of human presumption was heavy on both
the king and his spiritual counselor.

"The First Answer Was Me, the Second Was God"

Nathan's first response to David's question
came quickly—too quickly.

What would *you* say if a wealthy and powerful
head of state confided in you that he wanted to
build a worship center for God in your city—with
no strings attached and at no expense to anyone
except himself? Nathan said, "Yeah! Go for it! God
is with you!"

Leaders who often speak on God's behalf
when preaching the Word, counseling, or proph-
esying find it all too easy to speak for Him on matters about which they haven't asked God previously.

It isn't enough simply to measure whether or
not a thing seems to match up with basic scriptur-
al principles. This doesn't even begin to address

things such as timing, methodology, motives, or the intricate *details* of God's all-wise master plan for man.

Nathan, the man of God, probably felt confident that he had given God's opinion on David's proposition, but *that night* the prophet discovered that God had a *different* take on what David wanted to do.

> Go and tell David my servant, Thus saith the LORD, Thou shalt not build me an house to dwell in (1 Chronicles 17:4).

God wasn't angry or harsh. He didn't say, "Tell David, that wicked man" or "David the fool." He called David His servant; nevertheless, His answer was blunt: "You're not going to build me a house." This is a loving but firm *refusal*.

The fact that God said "no" isn't surprising. He often says "no." This time, however, God was saying "no" to David's *deepest, most loving desire!* And the king's desire wasn't even for himself; it seemed to be offered solely for God's pleasure and benefit.

Many years passed before David truly understood why his dream was denied. Now this is hard to take when it happens in *our* lives or ministries! However, understand that when God says "no" to you (and He certainly will if He hasn't said it already), it isn't for *living*, it is for *learning*. He doesn't intend for you to live out your life in a "divine no"; He wants you to *learn* from His "no" so He can entrust you with a holy "yes" that will affect your life and the lives of many other people! If He says "no" to you, it is so that He can say "yes" to you for a deeper, stronger, and *greater* purpose.

We know for certain that Solomon was not born when God delivered His "no" to David through Nathan the prophet. Mercifully, God planted yet another dream in David's heart at the end of that painful reply—a dream that would directly concern Solomon.

It is interesting that Nathan prophesied in 2 Samuel 7:16, "And thine house and thy kingdom shall be established for ever before thee: thy throne shall be established for ever." Even in that moment, God knew "the end from the beginning." He knew that David would step out on his royal balcony one spring morning in Jerusalem while his troops and commanders fought with Philistines on a distant battlefield.

With his sword hand empty, and his prayer life far less urgent in the peaceful environment of Jerusalem than in places of desperate war or personal survival—David, the Sweet Psalmist of Israel, wasn't singing or praying that morning. He was disconnected from his purpose, and therefore bored, listless, distracted, and at great risk.

From the high vantage point of his royal balcony, David's wandering eyes spied a married woman named Bathsheba bathing on her private porch (apparently unclothed and unaware of the royal "peeping tom" above her). The king shamelessly used his royal power to follow his inward lust into outright sin.

> And David sent messengers, and took her;
> and she came in unto him, and he lay with
> her; for she was purified from her unclean-
> ness: and she returned unto her house (2
> Samuel 11:4).

We will examine this all-too-common sin in detail later on, but let's just say that adultery was followed by pregnancy and then deception. When deception failed, David resorted to a cold-blooded murder plot, and the plot led to the deadly deed.

After Bethsheba's husband was murdered—incredibly, Uriah was actually one of David's "Thirty Mighty Men" (see 1 Chronicles 11:41, 2 Samuel 23:19)—David took Bathsheba as his wife when her mourning period was complete. She bore a child from her illicit union with David, and the child died. Then Bathsheba bore him another son named Solomon.

A key phrase appears at the end of this verse in Second Samuel: "and [David] called his name Solomon: *and the LORD loved him*" (2 Samuel 12:24—emphasis mine).

Nineteen years later, we find King David explaining his original vision for God's house to his teenage son, Solomon:

> "My son, I had it in my heart to build a
> house for the Name of the LORD my
> God. "But this *word of the LORD* came to
> me: 'You have shed much blood and
> have fought many wars. You are not to

11

build a house for my Name, because you have shed much blood on the earth in my sight. 'But you will have a son who will be a man of peace and rest, and I will give him rest from all his enemies on every side. His name will be Solomon, and I will grant Israel peace and quiet during his reign. 'He is the one who will build a house for my Name. He will be my son, and I will be his father. And I will establish the throne of his kingdom over Israel forever'" (1 Chronicles 22:7–10, NIV, emphasis mine).

The first thing you should realize about this promise from God is that only *part* of this promise applies to Solomon. David's earthly son *did* indeed build the temple of David's dreams, but he did not raise up the temple of God described in *this* vision.

Solomon's temple perished after only a very short period on the human table of history. And Solomon's unified throne didn't last much longer than his life did. It was Jesus, the "Son of David," the One called Immanuel, "God with Us," who gave His body as a living sacrifice to Gentile executioners at the demand of Jewish accusers.

It was God who raised up Jesus' body, God's house, three days after His crucifixion. It was through the resurrection of Jesus Christ that the throne of David's line was established forever!

You Are Not to Build a House for My Name

David had received a *dabar*, a Hebrew word translated as "word" (pronounced "dah-varr"). It means "a reasoned word" from God. David's revelatory understanding of God's "no" didn't come overnight, and it didn't come purely through instantaneous and supernatural impartation.

This understanding came through a divinely reasoned word of the Lord as David pondered God's spoken prophetic word, the written Word passed down from the patriarchs, and the principles he had learned over a lifetime of intimacy and obedience with the Lord.

David was in God's will and in the Lord's presence. He had passed from endless crises to glorious crowning, and he seemingly had everything. Yet, he came to understand that his past had *disqualified* him from certain tasks, including the task that had become the central dream and focus of his life.

God told King David that he had "shed much blood" and "fought many wars." It doesn't take much thought to understand that he had broken many hearts and caused untold stress on people in his time—on his *subjects* who risked (and lost) their lives to fight the wars and upon his *enemies*. He had shed a *lot* of blood and shattered the dreams of many.

The point is that even though David had received perhaps the most difficult "no" God had delivered in his life, he managed to *figure it out and accept God's verdict!*

Now he understood his role—he would have a key role, an important part in the longing of his heart, but *another* would complete the vision God had given him. In the words of W. Phillip Keller, "This was not the man nor the era for [the temple's] construction."[1]

Although David had defeated his major enemies at that time, the city of Jerusalem was not yet secure (see 1 Kings 5:3–4). It is clear that Jerusalem was still vulnerable. As T. F. Zimmerman so aptly states, "Ninety percent of the will of God is timing." The life of Abraham illustrates this point: Abraham knew the will of God—it was for him to have a son. A son born *out of* or *apart from* the timing of God yielded Ishmael. A son born *in* the will of God yielded Isaac.

Has This Happened in Your Life?

Have you offered God everything only to see Him "do" nothing and offer no clear word one way or the other? Perhaps you made your best offer:

- In ministry—"Open up a place, Lord—I'll serve."

- In missions—"Just tell me where, Lord—I'll go."

- In marriage—"Bring the right person, Lord—I'll do it."

- In the marketplace—"Prosper my business, Lord—I'll give."

It is important to understand the difference between perceiving a need and receiving a call. Just because you see a need does not mean you have a call. You need nothing less than a word from the Lord!

What *Not* to Do When God Says "No"

The first thing you need to know when God says "no" is what *not* to do. Any one of these things can spell disaster for you personally and in your ministry.

Never allow yourself to feel *resentful, rebellious,* or *rejected.*

Never compare yourself to others. The adversary of your soul will do his evil best to direct your attention and envy toward someone else who is going forward in ministry while you feel as if you are sliding backwards. He will highlight friends or classmates who are moving into missions while you are just spinning your wheels back home.

One of the toughest tests comes for single Christians who must deal with loneliness while their friends and contemporaries marry and begin raising families. Perhaps you are still wrestling with God's "no" concerning your business while others are enjoying great success in business.

Remember this truth when God says "no" to your dream:

- It is never between you and them,

- It is always and only between you and Him!

What You *Should* Do When God Says "No"

Begin with this simple truth: Even if God says no to your idea or proposal, realize that *"it was good that it was in your heart to do it"* (2 Chronicles 6:8).

It is better spiritually to be *a willing son or daughter* with a rejected dream than one who *refused* to follow, or who went *unwillingly*. Look at the worst-case scenario from God's viewpoint: although you may never preach or set foot on foreign soil as a missionary, you can *more than fulfill* the dream God put inside you!

Consider David again. In God's sight, David gained just as much glory for building the temple as his son, Solomon!

- It is good that God put it (your dream) there!

- The answer is not to get rid of the dream!

- The answer is to find out what is your part of its fulfillment!

Second, make sure you *raise spiritual sons and daughters* to take your dream to the next level! In other words, your dream may well require a *team* to reach fulfillment. Consider Solomon's restatement of his father's words:

16

But the LORD said to David my father,
Forasmuch as it was in thine heart to
build an house for my name, thou didst
well in that it was in thine heart:

Notwithstanding thou shalt not build the
house; but thy son which shall come
forth out of thy loins, he shall build the
house for my name (2 Chronicles 6:8–9).

Become a model in the lives of those who
could fulfill your dream. Live as though you are
there! Don't let the dream die! Hold it up before
God...and others!

Third, resolve to *"gather materials"* for the
builder or builders whom God will call to fulfill
your dream!

At the end of David's life, he was able to say
publicly with total peace and truthfulness, "Now I
have prepared with all my might for the house of
my God. . . . because I have set my affection to the
house of my God, I have of mine own personal
treasure . . . given over and above all that I have
prepared for the holy house" (1 Chronicles 29:2–3).

According to 1 Chronicles 26:26–28, King
David even set aside *one-fifth* of the spoils of war
with Israel's enemies to build God's temple.
According to Dr. Keller, at the time of his death,
"The total treasury assembled by David for the
temple exceeded *billions of dollars.*"[2]

What a splendid example! God said "no" to
David about the single greatest desire of his life,

17

but instead of quitting, becoming angry, or feeling sorry for himself, David gave his life wholeheartedly to the task and dream at the highest possible level.

What a lesson!

If you cannot build—you can gather!

If you cannot go—you can send!

If God says "no" to your dream, you make it possible for someone else to do what God put in your heart!

And finally . . .

Truly Hear and Recognize

What God Is Saying

When He Says "No"

Even when God says "no" to you, He whispers *regal reminders* and *precious promises* to your heart that will reassure you, even in your temporary disappointment. And in the end, they will produce *great gratitude* in a willing heart. God's work in David's life demonstrates the heavenly pattern perfectly.

David received a *regal reminder* in 2 Samuel 7:8–9, where God said He had taken David "from the sheepcote" (*naveh* in the Hebrew) and from following sheep to be ruler of His people. The *naveh* was the abode of a shepherd, not a son. David was sent out from the house of his wealthy family to do a hired man's work, but God pulled him in to be "a ruler" (*nagidh* or a leader in the Hebrew).

This regal reminder assured David that he had God's "unconditional acceptance," and you and I have it as well. David *needed* this reminder because his father, Jesse, had *rejected* him.

Jesse didn't bother to summon David to the house after the most revered prophet of his day commanded Jesse to brings his sons to a sacrifice (see 1 Samuel 16:5, 10–11). David was also forbidden to go into the army with his brothers (a place reserved for "sons" and not servants, freemen and not slaves), and David never mentions his mother's name. Nevertheless, God was saying, "I accept you!"

God reminded David that he enjoyed virtually unlimited favor with Him (and so do you if you pursue God as David did). The Lord was with him wherever he went, and He "cut off" David's enemies from his sight. Even more, God made David "a great name" (*shem* in the Hebrew, meaning "character, or inner-self), like ". . . the name of the great men that are in the earth" (2 Samuel 7:9).

God also reminded David of His five-part *precious promise* to him and his descendants. He promised David, ① "I will make you a house" (v. 11), and continued with this promise over his descendants: ② "I will set up your seed after you, who will come from your loins; and I will establish his kingdom" (v. 12).

The Lord then said this "seed of David" would "build a house for my name" (v. 13a), and promised that He would "establish the throne of his kingdom forever" (v. 13b). Again, remember that this prophetic statement could *not* apply to Solomon because it was directed toward Jesus!

Unlike Solomon, God Himself promised to be a father to this divine seed. Do you recall Jesus, the "Son of David," crying out to God in the garden of Gethsemane? He said, "Abba, *Father*, all things are possible unto thee; take away this cup from me: nevertheless not what I will, but what thou wilt" (Mark 14:36).

That "cup" was the suffering that specifically applied to this "seed of David."

> I will be his father, and he shall be my son. If he commit iniquity, I will chasten him with the rod of men, and with the stripes of the children of men (2 Samuel 7:14).

This prophecy through Samuel is an accurate portrait of "the Suffering Servant" also described prophetically in Isaiah 52–53. The good news is that the Lord also promised His "mercy shall not depart from him"!

In the fifth and final part of the promise, God said, "And your house and kingdom shall be established forever before you: your throne shall be established forever"(v. 16).

This is the defining moment of David's life!

What happened in David's life may happen in yours: *God says His "yes" in the midst of His "no."*

David said later of this word, "Thy word have I hid in my heart that I might not sin against Thee" (Psalm 119:11). And God also referred to this word through Luke's account in the Book of Acts, saying, "I have found David the son of Jesse, a man after mine own heart" (Acts 13:22). This is staggering! (It is also a divine restatement and expansion of God's ancient promise to Abraham from Genesis 15:1–21).

The Lord essentially told David, "You will be my house, but I am the Builder, not you. David, as you gather and give, I will grow and build you until *you* are all I have called you to be." The process is the *same* for you and me today! Christian scholar F. W. Krummacher noted in his landmark book, *David: King of Israel*: "This is the most important and surprising moment in David's life."[3]

A Great Gratitude

David's journey through the "no" of God finally produced *great gratitude*, especially when his understanding began to catch up with his loyal obedience and trust in God. The Bible tells us in dual accounts that King David "went in (before the ark), and sat before the Lord . . ." (2 Samuel 7:18, 1 Chronicles 17:16).

This is overwhelming. Four things roll up from deep inside him.

1. Who am I, Lord . . . that you have brought me this far? (v. 18)

2. Is this the manner of men, O Lord? (v. 19)

   If we look at David's life experiences, we have to say, "Evidently not!" David was betrayed by men such as his father, Jesse; by his king, Saul; by his eldest brother, Eliab; and by countrymen he labored to protect, such as Nabal. Unfortunately, men only bless people who, in their limited judgment and estimation, appear to be good and worthy people (or politically useful). God clearly sees things differently. As Hannah (Samuel's mother) said:

   He raiseth up the poor out of the dust, and lifteth up the beggar from the dunghill, to set them among princes, and to make them inherit the throne of glory . . ." (1 Samuel 2:8a, NIV).

3. And what can David [or Ron Cottle] say more to you? (v. 20)

   Like Job before him, David was saying, "I put my hand upon my mouth." This is too deep for words!

4. "The word which you have spoken concerning me, do it, Lord, as You said. Let the house

of Thy servant be established forever!" (vv. 25–29)

At this instant, David:

- **Confessed God's Promise . . .**

- **Claimed God's Word . . .**

- **Clenched God's Destiny.**

This is the moment David planted God's Word in his heart as the guiding principle of his life. It is no accident that in the end, it was God who wrote David's epitaph: "I have found David son of Jesse *a man after* [reaching for/reflecting from] *my own heart; he will do everything I want him to do"* (Acts 13:22, NIV).

How Does This Apply to You in Your Life?

1. Can you identify with this word?

2. Have you offered God your best and received His divine "no"?

3. If you have, then did you hear what He really said?

   I will:

   - *Take you farther.*
   - *Make you better.*
   - *Use you to a greater measure*

23

in My "no" than in My
"yes."

Just put it all in My hands.

Build My Kingdom, not your empire.

Seek significance, not success.

Then I will give you more than you can
ever thank Me for!

1. One by one He took them from me,
   All the things I valued most.
   Until I was empty-handed;
   Every glittering toy was lost.

2. And I walked earth's highways grieving,
   In my rags and poverty.
   Till I heard His voice inviting,
   Lift those empty hands to ME!

3. So I held my hands toward Heaven,
   And He filled them with a store
   Of His own transcendent riches
   Till they could contain no more.

4. And at last I comprehended
   With my stupid mind and dull,
   That God could NOT pour His riches
   Into hands already full.

Notes

1. W. Phillip Keller, *David, the Shepherd King*, Vol. 2 (Waco, Texas: Word Books, 1996), p. 61.

2. Keller, p. 63.

3. F. W. Krummacher, *David, King of Israel*. Trans. M. G. Easton (Grand Rapids, MI: Kregel Classics, 1994), p. 250. (Originally published by T&T Clark, Edinburgh.)

CHAPTER 2

THE POWER OF KEEPING COVENANT

David Keeps His Covenant with Mephibosheth

2 Samuel 9:1–13

> *David asked, "Is there anyone still left of the house of Saul to whom I can show kindness for Jonathan's sake?"* (2 Samuel 9:1, NIV)

What are some marks of a godly man? After David captured the whole land God purposed for His people to possess, drove out all of his enemies, and ruled as undisputed king over both Judah and the rest of Israel, he found himself enjoying great peace and provision from the Lord.

The Bible says, "David executed judgment and justice unto all his people, and the Lord preserved David wherever he went" (2 Samuel 8:15).

At that point, *King David did two things* that clearly mark him as a godly man. *First* he reflected on God's goodness and said, "What can I do for

God?" *Then* David remembered the covenant promise that *he* had made to his late friend, Jonathan; and he in essence asked, "What can I do for this covenant?"

Remember that David's life was marked by his interaction with a number of key people as he walked out his days with God. He wasn't perfect (and neither are we), but David's love for God and his intimate relationship with Him carried him through.

His actions toward *people* also marked him as God's anointed (and as a human being in need of God's mercy and grace). Author Alan Redpath considered this period after David assumed Israel's throne to be "the high point" of the Psalmist's life, his "greatest hour."[1] (While I do not feel it is the *highest* point in David's life, I do agree that it is one of the most important points in his life and ministry.)

We see God's redemptive plan from *two sides* when David extended his covenant promise made to Jonathan in specific application to Mephibosheth, Jonathan's only son and heir. Simultaneously we see the action of *a redeemer* (David) toward the redeemed (Mephibosheth); and the response of the *redeemed* toward the redeemer.

We can learn a great deal from Mephibosheth's life-altering encounter with David, his unlikely *kinsman-redeemer*. Let me urge you to begin the learning process with prayer: ask the Holy Spirit to alter *your* life as He reveals the truths pictured in Mephibosheth's *condition*, his *call*, and his *crown*.

Mephibosheth's Condition

> Jonathan son of Saul had a son who was
> lame in both feet. He was five years old
> when the news about Saul and Jonathan
> came from Jezreel. His nurse picked him
> up and fled, but as she hurried to leave,
> he fell and became crippled. His name
> was Mephibosheth (2 Samuel 4:4, NIV).

Why would a woman devoted to caring for
and protecting a young royal prince run in such
hurry and panic? It had to be serious enough for
her to risk her own life, because painful death was
the virtually certain sentence delivered for anyone
harming royalty in Bible times.

The panic and hysteria seem logical when we
realize that Mephibosheth was Jonathan's firstborn
son and the heir-apparent to the throne. That meant
that he became the sole remaining obstacle between
David and the throne of Israel that day when King
Saul and Crown Prince Jonathan fell in battle.

It was at King David's request that a surviving
servant from Saul's house name Ziba was brought
before David. Under questioning, Ziba revealed
that a son of Jonathan had miraculously survived,
and that Mephibosheth was a grown man, physi-
cally disabled, and living in desperate poverty and
obscurity.

If David had acted like any of the other kings
in neighboring nations or in human history up to
that time, then Mephibosheth probably wouldn't

have seen another sunset after his father's death. Even in a nation supposedly dedicated to God and His Law under Moses, everyone must have assumed that David, whom everyone knew God had chosen, would exterminate Mephibosheth.

Because Mephibosheth's nurse knew how badly Saul had treated David, it was natural for her to snatch up her five-year old charge and run in a panic. She had "insider" knowledge as a servant to the inner circle of Saul's royal family. She had been privy to countless retellings of the family history and to Saul's maniacal ravings over his frustrated attempts to exterminate David over the years. Surely David had a right to kill the heir of his most vicious and determined enemy now that the tide had turned.

In her haste, she stumbled and fell, permanently crippling Jonathan's sole heir. The boy seemed to disappear from sight and the biblical record for decades until the ninth chapter of the Book of Second Samuel.

David learns from Ziba that Mephibosheth was living in Lodebar, which in the Hebrew means "pastureless." This desolate area had *no pasture* to support life. It had *nothing*. It was literally *nowhere!* In Mephibosheth's mind, he must have given up all hope with the news that another had taken control of his rightful inheritance through his father and grandfather. (It was customary for the winner in royal disputes for control of a nation to seize all the lands and possessions of the loser.)

In the natural realm of physical senses and

human reasoning, this forgotten heir of a fallen royal house was just a *nobody* with *nothing* living in *nowhere*. In the realm of God and His Kingdom, Mephibosheth's life had a divine purpose. In fact, his very name means in the original Hebrew *dispeller of shame*.[2]

Mephibosheth had inherited a treasure he did not know about (because no one had told him). The treasure was a covenant of mutual protection and provision made between his father, Jonathan, and the new king, David, even before Mephibosheth's birth. It offered both heavenly and earthly benefits:

> "But if my father is inclined to harm you, may the LORD deal with me, be it ever so severely, if I do not let you know and send you away safely. . . . But show me unfailing kindness like that of the LORD as long as I live, so that I may not be killed, and do not ever cut off your kindness from my family— not even when the LORD has cut off every one of David's enemies from the face of the earth."
>
> *So Jonathan made a covenant with the house of David*, saying, "May the LORD call David's enemies to account." And Jonathan had David reaffirm his oath out of love for him, because he loved him as he loved himself (1 Samuel 20:13–17, NIV).

David actually reaffirmed this covenant with King Saul himself after David spared Saul's life in the cave. The embarrassed king said to David:

> When a man finds his enemy, does he let him get away unharmed? May the LORD reward you well for the way you treated me today. I know that you will surely be king and that the kingdom of Israel will be established in your hands. Now swear to me by the LORD that you will not cut off my descendants or wipe out my name from my father's family."
> So David gave his oath to Saul (1 Samuel 24:19–22a, NIV).

You and I also have a heavenly treasure we need to know about:

God, the King of Kings, cut a *covenant* with Jesus that can instantly transport us from *Lodebar* to the table of the King!

How many times do we live like paupers while our passport to the King's Table lies dormant and untapped? How many of us actually receive Jesus Christ and are "made the righteousness of God," yet continue to live as slaves to sin and failure?

Although our "grandfather" Adam fell in spiritual death and yielded his throne to Satan, Jesus restored us to the royal table and gave us rights and privileges as members of God's royal house. Yet we still live as if we are under Satan's rule and power!

Perhaps we should look closely at Mephibosheth's "qualifications" for being called to the king's house.

Mephibosheth's Call

David asked, "Is there anyone still left of the house of Saul to whom I can show kindness for Jonathan's sake?" (2 Samuel 9:1)

Sometimes we read God's Word too quickly and miss some life-altering truths. This passage seems to invite a speedy bypass while costing us invaluable wisdom. David's words echo the words of One who would follow him, of One who was much greater. Jesus, just as David did, calls out to *"anyone"* and *"everyone."*

Like David before Him, the divine Son of David calls out seeking those to whom He can show loving *hesed* (a Hebrew word meaning extraordinary and unmerited *mercy or grace*). When he asked for *anybody,* he did not specify that it had to be somebody who was "qualified." He didn't ask if anybody was "worthy," either. He simply asked, "Is there *anybody*?"

When Ziba, a former servant of Saul, finally stepped forward and said, "*Yes, there is someone,*" he felt he had to add, "*but he is crippled*" (see 2 Samuel 9:2–3). If you examine David's answer, you might notice that he didn't respond by asking, "How crippled?" He asked only, "Where is he located?" Ziba's answer could be the spiritual biography of every human being since Adam and Eve (although many would deny it on "good days").

Mephibosheth was . . .

- **In Nowhere!**
- **Alone . . . abandoned . . . alienated**
- **Broken . . . bitter . . . beaten**
- **Crippled . . . conflicted . . . crushed**
- **Defeated . . . destroyed . . . devastated**

David accomplished on a small scale what the "Son of David" accomplished on the cosmic scale when he called Mephibosheth *out of Lodebar*, out of nowhere, and brought him up to the king's table. But the transition was anything but smooth and worry-free. God offers us *no guarantees* that our transition from nowhere to His royal table will be trouble-free and painless.

The Bible says, "King David had him brought from Lo Debar, from the house of Makir son of Ammiel" (2 Samuel 9:5 NIV). What it *doesn't* say is how Mephibosheth felt about it all. We *do* have some hints, however.

Some commentators including Matthew Henry assume that David sent Mephibosheth's guardian, Makir, to retrieve him from Lodebar. But this is unlikely since it is clear that Mephibosheth was apprehensive about what awaited him in the King's court at Jerusalem. Makir would surely have gone to great lengths to calm Mephibosheth's fears if he had been assigned to bring Jonathan's son to Jerusalem. That leaves David's officials and soldiers to do the task.

Now just imagine what the sole living male descendant of King Saul felt like when David's soldiers—fresh from *years of exile and desperate flight* under Saul's cruel rule—knocked on the door of his wilderness refuge and said: *"The king wants to see you!"*

You don't have to be a genius or a prophet to realize Mephibosheth was in shock! A string of rapid-fire thoughts must have hurtled through his mind as adrenaline coursed through his body:

> "This is the end! I always thought it would come to this . . . no one can resist the force of God's favor on David. My father always said David was destined to be king—even though my grandfather was determined to block that destiny. My life may be miserable, but it seems even that was more than I deserved. Now I'm finished!"

Even the fact that he wasn't killed instantly probably didn't bring Mephibosheth much comfort. His mind must have worked through all of the possibilities awaiting him in the court of his grandfather's sworn enemy.

Would he die quickly, or would his end come slowly, painfully, and in full view of the king's court? Would his name become a byword for what happens to the enemies of Israel's newest king? After all, David was known as Israel's greatest and most deadly soldier, a man who knew how to kill in countless ways without pity or hesitation. It was said that tens of thousands of battle-hardened warriors had fallen at his hand. Now, with Mephibosheth's face being the last vestige of grandfather Saul's family line, would he be just the latest to fall under David's sword?

It seems possible that this drama played itself out continually in painful progression throughout the journey from Lodebar to Jerusalem. When the travelers finally reached the city and brought Mephibosheth into King David's presence, the actions of Jonathan's son speak for themselves. This man feared for his life.

> When Mephibosheth son of Jonathan, the son of Saul, came to David, he bowed down to pay him honor.
> David said, "Mephibosheth!"
> "Your servant," he replied (2 Samuel 9:6, NIV).

What could this mean? The *New Living Translation* says, "When he came to David, *he bowed low in great fear. . . ."*

Mephibosheth's Crown

Just imagine the rush Mephibosheth must have felt when he heard his name on the lips of the king who held the power of life and death over him! His response was both instant and dramatic.

The Bible says Mephibosheth "bowed down" before King David. This man didn't merely bow his knee before David; the Hebrew phrase used in the Bible tells us Mephibosheth virtually *threw himself down* to the floor and then he *prostrated himself face down* before David.[3]

Remember that nothing about Mephibosheth's physical infirmity had changed: this man was *carried* into the king's presence or, at the very best, he managed to move into the room on his own using a primitive form of crutches (remember, *both* of his feet had been so damaged that he couldn't walk). So Mephibosheth either *threw away* his crutches or *cast off* all assistance he may have received from other people—and he did it to fall down before the one who had all rights and sovereignty over his life. He wasn't brought before an elected president or an appointed prime minister—he was face-to-face with an ancient oriental king endowed with full rights of life and death over his subjects.

When King David said, *"Mephibosheth,"* it remains unclear from the original Hebrew writings whether he said it as a question or as an exclamation. In other words, we don't know if this frightened man was greeted with a voice emphasis that sounded like, "So, are *you* Mephibosheth?" or "S-o-o, *you* are this Mephibosheth I've heard about!"

Regardless of the answer, the man probably felt certain he was about to feel the cutting pain of a sword striking his neck. Mephibosheth immediately answered with words that might mean in modern English, "You are looking at your slave, your personal servant."[4]

His fear must have been visible without any words being said, because King David immediately spoke out to dispel Mephibosheth's fear.

> "Don't be afraid," David said to him, "for I will surely show you kindness for the sake of your father Jonathan. I will restore to you all the land that belonged to your grandfather Saul, and you will always eat at my table" (2 Samuel 9:7, NIV).

King David's three-part response to Mephibosheth literally foreshadows the Son of David's reply to all of us to bow before God as sinners in need of a Savior. He promised to *show kindness* (whether we deserve it or not), to *restore* everything lost due to sin and separation, and to *provide* for all of our needs. The king was saying to Jonathan's broken and fearful son, "Don't be afraid. I will show you grace because of the *covenant* I made with your father!"

Three Words Tell the Story of Mephibosheth — the Dispeller of Shame

This blessed moment in Mephibosheth's life is defined by three powerful words that paint a portrait of God-ordained restoration, hope, and renewal:

1. Acceptance

> "Don't be afraid," David said to him, "for I will surely show you kindness [*hesed* — mercy or grace] for the sake of your father Jonathan" (2 Samuel 9:7a, NIV).

David was saying to Mephibosheth, "I made a covenant with your father, Jonathan, that includes you — so I *accept you* in him!"

Do you realize that in His Word, God tells us, "I made a covenant with My Son, Jesus, that includes *you*" — so He *accepts us* in Him? The Bible says in Romans 5:10, "For if, when we were God's enemies, we were reconciled to him through the death of his Son, how much more, having been reconciled, shall we be saved through his life!" (NIV).

2. Abasement

> Mephibosheth bowed down and said, "What is your servant, that you should notice a dead dog like me?" (2 Samuel 9:8, NIV).

It may seem ironic, but the grace that David poured out freely on this broken man made him recognize his unworthiness and lowliness even more! It isn't unusual for people to feel totally unworthy when they first encounter the genuine love of Jesus and the grace of God. It happened in the Old Testament to great prophets and leaders such as Elijah and Moses; and it happened often in the New Testament. Grace always does that. Alan Redpath said, "Grace never leaves a man with his self-righteousness and pride."[5] Isaac Watts captured this magnificent moment in his hymn:

When I survey the wondrous cross

On which the Prince of glory died,

My richest gain I count but loss,

And pour contempt on all my pride.

3. Abundance

". . . I will *restore to you all the land* that belonged to your grandfather Saul, and you will *always eat at my table*" (2 Samuel 9:7b, NIV, emphasis mine).

Paul the apostle echoed a similar promise offering ever *greater* benefits to you and me because of the loving self-sacrifice of Jesus Christ, called "the Son of David." God's promise to us does more than elevate us to dine at His divine table; He literally makes us "sit together" enthroned in heavenly places with our Lord Jesus Christ! The apostle said:

But because of his great love for us, God, who is rich in mercy. . . . raised us up with Christ and seated us with him in the heavenly realms in Christ Jesus, in order that in the coming ages he might show the incomparable riches of his grace, expressed in his kindness to us *in Christ Jesus* (Ephesians 2:4, 6–7, NIV, emphasis mine).

King David's covenant promise to Mephibosheth, Jonathan's heir who had been self-exiled to the barren nowhere place called "pastureless," was repeated *four times*:

- 2 Samuel 9:7—"And you shall eat bread at my table continually."

- 2 Samuel 9:10—"But Mephibosheth your master's son shall eat bread at my table always."

- 2 Samuel 9:11—"As for Mephibosheth," said the king, "he shall eat at my table like one of the king's sons."

- 2 Samuel 9:13—"So Mephibosheth dwelt in Jerusalem, for he ate continually at the king's table."

King David honored his covenant promise to Jonathan by bringing his son, Mephibosheth, up from "Nowhere" to take his lifelong seat at the king's banqueting table. He, for all intents and purposes, made Mephibosheth a son of the king.

Take a moment to picture in your mind what life was like at the king's supper table. Now picture what it *will* be like for *you* at the King of King's supper table in heaven! This is what Jesus has accomplished for you! Don't let it be for nothing. Don't let it take you nowhere.

1. You do not have to remain in Lo-debar, the pastureless, fruitless place of no hope.

2. You can eat and live at the King's table.

3. Now accept and enter into what Jesus has done for you!

Notes

1. Alan Redpath, *The Making of a Man of God* (Grand Rapids, MI: Fleming H. Revell, 1962), p. 185.

2. *Biblesoft's New Exhaustive Strong's Numbers and Concordance with Expanded Greek-Hebrew Dictionary* (Copyright © 1994, 2003 Biblesoft, Inc. and International Bible Translators, Inc.), s.v. OT:4648, *Mephiybosheth* (mef-ee-bo'-sheth); or Mephi-bosheth (mef-ee-bo'-sheth); probably from OT:6284 and OT:1322; *dispeller of shame* (i.e. of Baal); Mephibosheth, the name of two Israelites,"

3. Ibid. Refers to three phrases/words in combination: OT:5307, *naphal*, with several meanings, including "to cast down self" and "to throw down"; OT:6440, *paniym* (paw-neem'), referring to the "face"; and OT:7812, *shachah* (shaw-khaw'); "a primitive root; to depress, i.e. prostrate (especially reflexive, in homage to royalty or God): to bow (self) down, crouch, fall down (flat), humbly beseech, do (make) obeisance, do reverence, make to stoop, worship."

4. Ibid., s.v. OT:5647, `abad (aw-bad'); "a primitive root; to work (in any sense); by implication, to serve, till, (causatively) enslave, etc.: KJV - be, keep in bondage, be bondmen, bond-service, compel, do, dress, ear, execute, husbandman, keep, labour (-ing man, bring to pass, (cause to, make to) serve (-ing self,), (be, become) servant (-s), do (use) service, till (-er), transgress [from margin], (set a) work, be wrought, worshiper."

5. Redpath, p. 189.

CHAPTER 3

THE POWER OF FOCUS

*From Insult to Greatness: David's Greatest
War-time Victory*

2 Samuel 10:1–6

In the course of time, the king of the
Ammonites died, and his son Hanun succeeded
him as king.

David thought, "I will show kindness to
Hanun son of Nahash, just as his father showed
kindness to me." So David sent a delegation to
express his sympathy to Hanun concerning his
father.

When David's men came to the land of the
Ammonites, the Ammonite nobles said to Hanun
their lord, "Do you think David is honoring your
father by sending men to you to express sympathy? Hasn't David sent them to you to explore the
city and spy it out and overthrow it?"

So Hanun seized David's men, shaved off half
of each man's beard, cut off their garments in the
middle at the buttocks, and sent them away.

When David was told about this, he sent messengers to meet the men, for they were greatly humiliated. The king said, "Stay at Jericho till your beards have grown, and then come back."

When the Ammonites realized that they had become a stench in David's nostrils, they hired twenty thousand Aramean foot soldiers from Beth Rehob and Zobah, as well as the king of Maacah with a thousand men, and also twelve thousand men from Tob (2 Samuel 10:1–6, NIV).

Hunan is yet another man whose interaction with King David helped mark and frame his legacy as "a man after God's own heart." Hanun's name literally means "to stoop and to serve." Unfortunately, this young Ammonite king didn't live up to his name. His rash act of presumption and pride cost the lives of sixty thousand warriors and placed all of Ammon and its allies under the rule of King David.

Ammon was one of six hostile "tribute" peoples of whom David said, "They compassed me about *like bees*" (Psalm 18:12). The Philistines were to the southwest, the Amalekites and Edomites were to the south, the Moabites to the southeast, Ammon was to the north, and the Syrians were north of Ammon.

The Ammonites were a nomadic desert race descended from Ben-Ammi, Lot's younger son by his daughter.[1] The Ammonites were "second cousins" to the Israelites through Abraham's nephew, but they refused to help the Israelites when they fled Egypt. They often sided against Israel with the Moabites. who even hired the false prophet Balaam hoping he would prophesy against and curse Israel.

Things hadn't changed much in Ammonite sentiments by the time Israel installed a tall young man named Saul as its first king.

Hanun's father, Nahash, was king of Ammon during Saul's reign. He was considered cruel and formidable, and he openly threatened the Israelite city of Jabesh-Gilead in 1 Samuel 11.

When the city appealed to Saul for help, Israel's first king mustered his reluctant army through fear rather than relationship. He sent butchered slabs of beef to leaders around the nation along with a threat: he would butcher *their* cattle if they did not come to fight Nahash and the Ammonites.

Within twenty-four hours, Saul crossed the Jordan River by cover of night with his new (but reluctant and untrained) army. He successfully launched a surprise attack on Ammon that routed their army.[2]

Even though the Ammonites hated Saul and opposed Israel, King Nahash must have established a friendship or working relationship with David during his flight from King Saul and his men. We don't know if King Nahash gave David information, supplies or even safe refuge from Saul. The Bible simply reveals David's pure motivation with

47

the words, "David thought, 'I will show kindness to Hanun son of Nahash, *just as his father showed kindness to me*'" (2 Samuel 10:2, italics mine).

It seems that young Prince Hanun had spent more time running with his young friends than learning the secrets of leadership at his father's side, because he seemed to know nothing about his father's personal (and possibly *secret*) relationship with David. His disconnected relationship with his father and the apparent unavailability or disregard for seasoned counsel from older nobles set the stage of his life for certain disaster.

When Ammon's King Nahash died, his son Hanun took the throne and encircled himself with noble counselors. It seems, judging by their hot-headed advice, that these men were hand-picked from his younger circle of nobles.

When King David sent a royal delegation to Ammon as a sign of respect and condolence to King Hanun after his father's death (2 Samuel 10:1–2), David's act of kindness created the opportunity for royal insult by King Hanun.

Enter the rash young counselors with tragedy in their words. When King Hanun asked for advice from these nobles, they displayed their ignorance of history and of the international balance of power. They believed David's act of kindness was merely a trick to spy out the city. In the end, Hanun chose youthful but uninformed bravado over mature caution. (Surely he had heard about David's military exploits at some time in his lifetime!)

> When David's men came to the land of
> the Ammonites, the Ammonite nobles
> said to Hanun their lord, "Do you think
> David is honoring your father by send-
> ing men to you to express sympathy?
> Hasn't David sent them to you to explore
> the city and spy it out and overthrow it?"
> So Hanun seized David's men, shaved off
> half of each man's beard, cut off their gar-
> ments in the middle at the buttocks, and
> sent them away (2 Samuel 10:2b–4, NIV).

Unwise advice is always costly, but it is especially dangerous for those steering the national
affairs of state in precarious times. Hanun made
the biggest mistake of his young life, and it was
about to abort his future and inflict his people with
massive loss of life and freedom.

King Hanun ordered the arrest of King David's
royal peace ambassadors, and then insulted them
by shaving off half of each man's beard, and by
cutting off half of their official robes at the buttocks! These were ultimate acts of disgrace and
humiliation in that day.

A man's beard in bibilical times was a sign of
virility, wisdom, and honor. To cut off or disfigure
a man's beard against his will was a personal insult
against the man and his family. To desecrate the
official robes of a king's royal ambassador was considered to be an insult and international crime
against the king himself. It *still* is in modern times.

Did you ever wonder why King Herod's soldiers and the Roman executioners specifically "plucked out" Jesus' beard? It was their way of inflicting *severe insult and humiliation* to the One who was called King of the Jews. These hardened professional soldiers didn't merely cut off Jesus' beard; they brutally *pulled out* parts of His beard, leaving Him bloodied and disfigured to the highest degree.

When King David learned what happened, he sent messengers to his humiliated representatives and told them to *"remain in Jericho until your beards be grown."*

The news soon crossed the River Jordan that Israel's powerful King David was preparing for vengeance (that was how pagan kings would view it—in God's eyes it would be justice). Nations share something in common with individuals (and even children in a school yard). Once the news spreads that bullies can have their way with someone who is weak or compliant, the bully line starts forming.

Many modern nations have acted decisively to protect ambassadors from attack overseas, or to rebuke insulting actions or harmful incursions by presumptuous nations seeking greater power or leverage internationally.

King Hunan's outrageous actions amounted to an insult King David was not willing to overlook. Even in our day, the nation of Israel has made it national policy to respond instantly and forcefully to nearly every attack against her citizens in Israel and abroad. It is the only reason that tiny nation has survived while surrounded on all sides by bitter, ancestral enemies with powerful, antagonistic allies. Its leaders are drawing their policy from King David's playbook.

No one realized just how David's bold response would wreak havoc on the young king who misread kindness. (Had this king studied history in his region, *perhaps* he could have avoided tragedy—but as we shall see, it seems God's hand was in this incident for greater purposes.) Sixty-thousand men would die defending Ammon, and all of those who lived in that nation or were allies would become slaves.

David's Angry Response

David's anger raged against the Ammonites and he determined to bury their rotten flesh in their own desert sands. The Lion of Judah was roused to attack, and even the dense leaders of the Ammonites knew they had better seek help. By one estimate, the King of Ammon spent about ten million dollars for mercenaries!

This is a grim commentary on the power of the imagination.

Early in "the Book of Beginnings," in Genesis 6:5, the Creator looked at the human race a relatively few generations after the fall of man in the Garden, and He ". . . saw that the wickedness of man was great in the earth, and that *every imagination of the thoughts of his heart was only evil continually*" (emphasis mine).

King David wrote in Psalm 62:3, "How long will ye *imagine mischief* against a man? ye shall be slain all of you: as a bowing wall shall ye be, and as a tottering fence" emphasis mine).

The Bible again confirms its status as God's Good News when it tells us how to deal with our imaginations through the apostle Paul's second letter to the church at Corinth:

> (For the weapons of our warfare are not carnal, but mighty through God to the pulling down of strong holds;)
>
> *Casting down imaginations*, and every high thing that exalteth itself against the knowledge of God, and bringing into captivity every thought to the obedience of Christ (2 Corinthians 10:4–5, emphasis mine).

No one is immune to the virus of vain imagination and presumption.

This is why you must have your mind *renewed*, even after you receive Jesus Christ as Lord and Savior!

> I beseech you therefore, brethren, by the mercies of God, that ye present your bodies a living sacrifice, holy, acceptable unto God, which is your reasonable service.
>
> And be not conformed to this world: but *be ye transformed by the renewing of your*

mind, that ye may prove what is that good, and acceptable, and perfect, will of God (Romans 12:1–2, emphasis mine).

In his letter to the Colossian church, Paul expands his explanation of how you *renew your mind* after your initial salvation experience:

Lie not one to another, seeing that ye have put off the old man with his deeds;

And have put on the new man, which is *renewed in knowledge* after the image of him that created him (Colossians 3:9–10, emphasis mine).

The Result of Insult: From Skirmish to All-Out War

Once Ammon's young king committed his international insult, Israel's seasoned warrior-king decided to send his chief general to handle the problem. So *Joab began the battle* because King David apparently considered it to be a mere regional skirmish. Surely General Joab and a small fraction of Israel's army could quickly put down this minor impudent king.

Everything changed when King Hunan panicked and drew in military reinforcements from Syria, Zobah and Aram (Mesopotamia). These were vassal states under Israel, subjugated national powers that saw a real chance to break free and took it!

Old General Joab was surprised that he had virtually two armies to fight, but he wasn't alarmed. In fact, I suspect the ruthless professional soldier in Joab relished the prospect of a challenging personal battle. He was a legend in his day, a "Goliath" in his own right, known far and wide among the regional nations as a cruel and deadly efficient killing machine.

Like so many professional assassins and battle-hardened soldiers over the centuries, Joab lived for mortal combat. He would kill without mercy or regret—just follow his career in the Old Testament record and you will understand what I'm saying.

King David kept this man close to him as his military commander for nearly forty-nine years, *even though* he could be classified as one of David's worst enemies most of that time—a man who was constantly plotting and scheming for his own purposes against the king.

Why did David tolerate this man? Because he was a military legend who *won his spurs* in David's army through unmatched courage, boldness, and military precision. What he *lacked* is what David had, however—*an intimate relationship with God, along with the divine anointing and favor* that comes with it. (Isn't this what made the difference in David's early battle with Goliath?)

Why am I going into such detail concerning Joab's reputation? It played a key role in what happened in this misunderstood "regional skirmish."

General Joab confronted his two-front military challenge by dividing his army into two parts. He reserved the more formidable force of Syrian troops for himself and his better-trained and battle-hardened troops, and placed the less experienced soldiers under Abishai to fight the Ammonites.

The Syrians were no match for Joab. In fact, they quickly fled from the field at the mere sight of Joab the Battlefield Legend. He won the "battle" with the Syrians without firing a single arrow or striking one blow with sword or spear!

Once the Ammonites saw their stronger Syrian allies turn tail and run; they adopted the same strategy. They ran back into their fortified city without even engaging Abishai and his troops.

When his enemies vanished, Joab decided his job was done and he returned to Jerusalem in triumph for a great celebration. The only problem was that the Syrians were *not* finished. The Syrian commanders must have decided to "retreat that day so they could fight another day." They promptly recruited many more mercenaries and mounted an insurrection against Israel on a *major* multi-national scale.

The War Is Waged

Once King David learned about the full-scale war escalating to the north of Israel, he put the nation on full war alert and ordered every member of Israel's army into the battle—all three hundred thousand of them. Unlike King Saul before him, all David had to do was say the word and his nation quickly answered his royal call to war.

This time, King David personally led the army into battle. There was one *greater than Joab* here, a prophet, priest, and king whose God went before and behind him in battle. The result was a stunning military victory in which sixty thousand warriors from Syria and her allies were killed and the back of the insurrection was totally broken.

In the end, Syria asked for terms of surrender and her citizens became slaves of Israel. Every nation and kingdom in that region of the world learned that mighty Syria—the perpetual marauder and bully of the Middle East—had became a vassal state paying tribute to Israel.

For the first time in his life and in the history of his young nation, David the shepherd-king had defeated all his enemies and inherited the ancient promise God gave to Abraham:

> In the same day the LORD made a covenant with Abram, saying, Unto thy seed have I given this land, from the river of Egypt unto the great river, the river Euphrates (Genesis 15:18).

It was ironic. At the conclusion of this war that King David had neither anticipated or wanted, he now stood at the pinnacle of his greatness as a warrior. For the first time in the history of the Israelite people, they collectively possessed full control of the geographical borders God prophesied would be theirs long before; and *all* of their enemies were under their rule.

Now it was time for King David to *execute judgment and justice unto all his people* as a statesman.[3]

The Final Consequences: David's Steps to Greatness

It is one thing to conquer lands and people. It is entirely another thing to hold them securely and maintain order. King David was about to establish *order* in the three principal areas of his life and rule under God's hands.

His first step was to set in order the *government* of the palace. In other words, David brought **personal order** into his own life and leadership inner circle.

At this point—well past his early struggles simply to survive—he began to think about legacy and history. That is why he appointed Jehoshaphat, the son of Ahilud, as *"recorder."* Jehoshaphat's job was to record or write down the chronicles or history of the kingdom.

David also appointed Seraiah as *"scribe"* or royal secretary. Under David, this office may have been equivalent in rank to a modern secretary of state for a nation; and the title originally described the military function of numbering or mustering the troops of a nation.[4]

Then King David appointed Benaiah, the son of Jehoida, as chief over the Cherethites (executioners) and the Pelethites (bodyguards). These two groups were the *"Captains of the Guard,"* the army within the army that always surrounded the monarch. (It was generally limited to six hundred men willing to fight to the death to protect the king—much as modern Secret Service officers in the United States take an oath to protect the President even at the cost of their own lives if necessary). Years later, Benaiah would also became head of the army under Solomon.

The second step King David took was to set in order the **worship** of the Tabernacle. In other words, he brought **spiritual order** to the nation (much as the Son of David, Jesus the Messiah, later brought divine order to the Kingdom of God on earth).

Since the temple hadn't yet been built in Jerusalem at that time, the old tabernacle at Gibeon was still in operation. King David appointed Zadok to lead worship at that location. He also appointed Abimelech, the son of Abiathar[5] the high priest (who was still serving David at that point), to officiate in the new tabernacle on Mt. Zion.

Finally, King David set in order the matters of state, and thus the third area of his rule came into focus when David brought **national order**.

David began the transformation from the administration handed down from Saul's reign to one of his own choice by personally appointing his sons to the highest offices of the state.

Some people may frown on this as "nepotism," or family favoritism. However, when a family is godly, then the ability to present a unified front to enemies and establish a godly succession and cross-generational multiplication of righteousness should be seen as the Lord's blessing.

The wonderful thing about "sons and daughters" in the Kingdom of God is that we are not limited purely to our physical descendants. Even a quick glance at the letters of Paul, a bachelor for life, reveals that he had many "spiritual sons" who received and carried on his "spiritual DNA."

The promise of descendants or children as divine gifts is is a key part of God's great promise to Abraham, in which God said:

> "I will surely bless you and make your descendants as numerous as the stars in the sky and as the sand on the seashore. Your descendants will *take possession of the cities of their enemies,* and through your offspring all nations on earth will be blessed, because you have obeyed me" (Genesis 22:17–18, NIV, emphasis mine).

It was King Solomon, King David's son, who wrote in Psalm 127:

> Sons are a heritage from the LORD,
>   children a reward from him.
>
> Like arrows in the hands of a warrior
>   are sons born in one's youth.
>
> Blessed is the man
>   whose quiver is full of them.
>   They will not be put to shame

*when they contend with their enemies
in the gate* (Psalm 127:3–5, NIV,
emphasis mine).

True sons and daughters of the heart and spirit make a great difference in the life and effectiveness of any great leader. In David's case, his sons literally *"stood before the king."*

The throne rooms of ancient kings were carefully controlled areas where access was rigidly screened and controlled for purposes of security and efficiency. Only the king's sons and a few other trusted counselors such as certain prophets, the high priest, and ranking military leaders had direct access into the king's presence.

In our day, access to the Oval Office of the President of the United States is carefully controlled and monitored. The same is true if you want to see the Prime Minister or the Queen or King of Great Britain, or primary leaders of any other nation on earth.

The Bible reveals the great privilege you and I enjoy today as adopted sons and daughters of God, with total and instant *access* to the presence of Almighty God. It is written in at least two places:

. . . those who are led by the Spirit of God
are sons of God. For you did not receive
a spirit that makes you a slave again to
fear, but you received the Spirit of son-
ship. And by him we cry, "Abba, Father."
The Spirit himself testifies with our spir-

it that we are God's children (Romans 8:14-16, NIV).

Because you are sons, God sent the Spirit of his Son into our hearts, the Spirit who calls out, "Abba, Father." So you are no longer a slave, but a son; and since you are a son, God has made you also an heir (Galatians 4:6-7, NIV).

Finally, it was known throughout David's kingdom that *anyone who sought an audience with the king* must do so through his sons. The Bible reveals that you and I have access to God our Father *only* through His only begotten Son, Jesus Christ. There is no other way, door, path, or procedure of access. Jesus is the Way and the Door to God's presence. There is no other.

Final Conclusion: From Insult to Greatness

Life lived in the pursuit of God and His Kingdom is anything *but* predictable. God has a way of causing even seemingly simple situations to lead us back to Him for fresh understanding, guidance, and strength. Never go merely with what you see, but take it first to Him "on bended knee." David's countless battles were marked by countless times of prayer and inquiry before the Lord. The Psalms of David are often literal "journal pages" of David's daily walk with God.

This incident involving a youthful insult from

a newly crowned king of Syria became **an instrument** *in the hands of God* to engineer David's greatest victory as king over Israel.

The Bible declares in Paul's epistle to the church at Philippi, "... for *it is God who works in you* to will and to act according to his good purpose" (Philippians 2:13, NIV, emphasis mine). God was at work—even using the proud and presumptuous insult of a pagan king—to bring His chosen servant to ever greater and higher dimensions of rule!

Perhaps you are facing a conflict or challenge in life that looked as if it would be "easy" to solve. However, it has become a nightmare that is pushing you to the limits of your patience and resources! You only need to know *two things* in any situation to make it through to the other side: (1) that God loves you, and (2) that your life is firmly in His hands.

Once you settle those crucial questions, you allow God to craft an instrument of victory from *every* situation in your life—even those that seem to be "losses." This is what is meant in the Book of Romans where it says, "And we know that *all things* work together *for good* to them that love God, to them who are the called according to his purpose" (Romans 8:28, emphasis mine).

David's secret to surviving impossible situations was no secret at all: he kept his focus on the Answer, the Lord, and not on his questions or ever-changing circumstances.

Notes

1. See Genesis 19:30–38 and Deuteronomy 2:19.

2. It seems Jabesh-Gilead never forgot Saul's good deed for them. When Saul and his son, Jonathan, fell in battle on Mt. Gilboa, representatives from this city recovered their bodies from the streets of the Philistine city of Beth Shan. Later, they released the bones of the deceased king and crown prince to King David for burial in Jerusalem.

3. First Chronicles 20–27 gives details of this period of David's life.

4. As referenced under "scribes" variously in M. G. Easton's *Illustrated Bible Dictionary*, 3rd ed. (Harper & Brothers, 1903); *Nelson's Illustrated Bible Dictionary* (Nashville, TN: Thomas Nelson Publishers, 1986); and A. R. Fausset's *Illustrated Bible Dictionary* (BibleSoft Electronic Database, 2003).

5. It is ironic that Abimelech's name, also spelled "*Ab-i-melek*" contains the root words *Ab* (Hebrew and Aramaic for "Father"); *i* or "my"; and *melek* , or "king." So Abimelech's name literally meant "my father is king." There was one glaring problem about that name—his father *was not* king over Israel. That could be embarrassing for the son of a priest serving under the rule of a *king*. Perhaps it was a

63

prophetic indication of the misplaced inten-
tions of Abimelech's father, Abiathar. This man,
Abiathar, would make a major mistake later in
his actions toward God's anointed king (see 1
Kings 1).

CHAPTER 4

SUCCESS, THE GREAT SEDUCER

(David's Darkest Hour)

2 Samuel 11

> *"The better the man the dearer the price he pays for a short season of sinful pleasure."*
>
> —F. B. Meyer

Even the "man after God's own heart" fell captive to sin's compulsive seduction for a brief season. Sadly, the relatively few days he spent in willful sin produced pain and sorrow for many *generations* of David's family line.

We can *learn vital lessons* from David's life choices and their far-reaching consequences in almost every area of his life.

The most sordid chapter in David's life appears in 2 Samuel 11, but before we examine the greatest failure of "the Sweet Psalmist of Israel," you should understand two important things about this chapter that directly impact *your own* life today.

First, you must notice and appreciate the absolute integrity of the Bible.

It would have been much "easier" for God to simply omit this awful act from the sacred drama of one of His greatest earthly heroes.

In fact, the official chronicles or written national history of this period of David's empire *do* omit the story (see 1 Chronicles 20–21). God, in effect, provided Israel with both "secular" government through the king and "spiritual" government through the prophets and His Word at the time.

The primarily *historical* books of the Chronicles bypass David's personal failures and focus instead upon David's governmental error in taking a census of the nation in disobedience to God, along with the punishment that followed.

The *prophetic voice* infusing First and Second Samuel conveys *every detail* of David's dramatic spiral into sin's arms. The unsparing honesty of the sacred text tears away every covering from David's personal life. We are forced to realize that even the very best among us is far from perfect. God alone is good; *all* men and women are sinners in need of grace.

Second, it is not the *hard times* in life that tend to defeat a person—most often you will come through times of hunger, struggle, and pain even stronger than before you encountered them. No, the most dangerous times in your life will be the *easy times*—the times of your life or ministry are marked by fullness, ease, and an abundance of pleasure or "spare time."

David did not fail God in the cave Adullam. The loneliness, danger, and lack he suffered during those years of exile only drove him to his knees and closer to God's presence. The shepherd boy didn't lose his grip while standing before Goliath, or as an exile prince and rejected son-in-law risking life and limb to avoid the armies of the bitter King Saul. In those moments, his soul soared in utter dependence and reliance upon the invisible God.

No, David's great fall came in those relaxed moments when he paused from his pursuit of God's purposes to luxuriate in his military victories, to soak in the adulation of the people, and to exalt in the sumptuousness of his palace.

For David, and for millions of men and women after him, it was *"success the great seducer"* that drew out that hidden pride and sense of elite superiority that brought him down. If *you* are a man or woman of destiny in God, then He is out to deal with your sin problem *now*. He will use adversity to test and strengthen your faith; but He may use success to probe your heart and life for that *hidden* sin that could bring you down. (Of course, no sin is really *hidden* from God, but unfortunately we nearly always *think* it is. As long as sin remains, then the possibility and probability of a fall is constantly growing inside us like a cancer.)

The "bell for hell" must have tolled loudly as the words were written in 2 Samuel 11, "In the spring, at the time when *kings* go off to war, David sent *Joab* . . ." (2 Samuel 11:1, NIV).

Once the person God anointed to lead Israel stopped moving forward and sent another in his place to oversee what he as a *king* usually tended to personally, he stopped growing in God. (This is different from proper delegation, an essential part of mature leadership. This may well have been dereliction of duty, given what happened afterward.)

David suddenly found his warrior hands empty with nothing to do and nothing to conquer . . . except another man's wife. Left at home alone while his men were dealing with the challenges and dangers of war, David no longer needed to lean on God as he usually did. He took time to listen and began to believe what others said about him being special, different, and deserving of more rights, privileges, and perquisites than others.

An old English proverb wisely warns us, "An idle mind is the devil's workshop." When David opened his mind and heart to thoughts of self-inflation and lust, his fall was imminent and inevitable.

If David, the legendary "man after God's own heart," could suddenly fall so far so quickly from such a monumental place of accomplishment and divine favor, then you and I *must* discover how to *avoid* the same fate!

This season is David's darkest but most illuminating moment in life. As we examine each step David took into self-destruction and calamity, we must remember a fundamental truth of life:

"Everything you do

strengthens or *weakens*

everything else you do."

We are about to highlight the "Three C's" of David's calamity—the *contributions* to his calamity, the *character* of this calamity, and finally, the terrible *consequences* of his calamity. Never was the quote by F. B. Meyer truer than in this tale of David's descent into sin: *"The better the man the dearer the price he pays for a short season of sinful pleasure."*

Contributions to David's Calamity

What were some of the *contributions* to David's calamity? First, we see that his personal *temperament* contributed greatly to David's fall. It is important to understand ourselves and to take an accurate and honest assessment of our nature and personal shortcomings.

The apostle Paul said, "Do not think of yourself more highly than you ought, but rather *think of yourself with sober judgment*, in accordance with the measure of faith God has given you" (Romans 12:3, NIV, emphasis mine).

In David's case, it appears from the portrait of Scripture that King David was a warm, poetic, and passionate person. A man like this is more *vulnerable* than some others to the particular sins of passion and lust. I still remember a man of a

69

very different temperament once telling me, "My Achilles' heel is not sex, it is *power!*" Had this particular man been confronted with the same temptation David faced on his roof so long ago, he would have said, "That woman just needs to get some clothes on. What is wrong with her?" He *knew* his own area of weakness. Do you?

Another major contributor to David's downfall was his very *success* or prosperity! Even the Church struggles greatly with this area—where believers fight the good fight of faith simply to survive and overcome ongoing persecution, the Church often prospers and glows with the life of God. Where believers generally have all of their needs met and face few problems or persecutions (in the United States for instance), the Church seems to struggle with endless distractions of the flesh and defeats over conflicts in the daily appointment calendar.

David had enjoyed seventeen years of *unbroken victory* on the battlefield during his twenty year reign! When you consider just how unpredictable and violent war has been historically, and realize that much of the time David and his men were outnumbered and under-equipped underdogs, you begin to understand his great accomplishments.

Unfortunately, the flip side of success can be dangerous. Every successful battle increased David's level of public adulation and it ultimately led to a sense of *superiority*. In a pattern we still see in political, sports, and religious leaders today, it appears that David came to "*believe his press*." It seems that he began to believe he was special and somehow *deserved* all this blessing.

While building the nation of Israel, King David broke some of God's clearly stated rules and requirements outlined in Deuteronomy 17:14–17:

"When you enter the land . . . [you will have a king] . . . ."

1. He shall not multiply *horses* unto himself.

2. He shall not multiply *wives* unto himself.

3. He shall not greatly increase *silver and gold* unto himself.

According to 2 Samuel 5:13, shortly after David was crowned king in Jerusalem, he *". . . took more concubines and wives from Jerusalem . . . ."* So while David kept the first and third requirement, he blatantly *ignored* the second. Remember, again, that *"Everything you do strengthens or weakens everything else you do."*

As we noted earlier, there is truth in the old English proverb, *"An idle mind is the devil's workshop." Leisure* in excess and the blind pursuit of pleasure is another contributor to calamity. Everyone needs to observe a sabbath for the body and soul, but idleness only contributes problems to your life.

Proverbs 21:17 warns, *"He that loves pleasure shall be a poor man.* And the Apostle Paul, writing about the dangers facing young marriageable widows, said, "Whereas she who lives in pleasure and self-gratification [giving herself up to luxury and self-indulgence] is dead even while she [still] lives" (1 Timothy 5:6, AMP).

Moses is one biblical leader who took the high road where idleness and ease are concerned.

> By faith Moses, when he had grown up, refused to be known as the son of Pharaoh's daughter. He chose to be mistreated along with the people of God rather than to enjoy the pleasures of sin for a short time (Hebrews 11:24–25, NIV).

The Character of David's Calamity

Some of the most popular counsel offered on national TV talk shows and pop-counseling radio shows takes the form of well-deserved self-indulgence. "You deserve it—take care of yourself. Pamper yourself. Put yourself *first* for a change . . . let everybody else wait and step back."

It sounds good, but it produces evil. It is true we should love ourselves and do what is necessary to take care of our health and wellbeing. But indulgence and self-centeredness only lead to trouble. There are four key choices that reveal the character flaws leading to David's calamity.

First, *David indulged himself. His self indulgence nearly aborted his promise* from God and almost wrecked his legacy.

1. He should have been in battle, but he stayed in his bedroom.

2. He should have been fighting in the trenches, but he rested on his laurels.

3. He should have been busy for God in that season, but he had leisure for self.

4. As a result, he was ripe for a fall when he walked onto the palace balcony and saw a beautiful woman bathing herself in plain view on her rooftop patio.

It is true that Bathsheba was not without fault in this setup for immorality. The place for a private bath is *inside* away from the public eye, not *outside* where anyone with a higher vantage point can see everything. If David could see *her* balcony, then without doubt Bathsheba could see him on *his* balcony. However, that does not excuse David.

Secondly, *David ignored all the warnings.* James warns us from his apostolic epistle to the church of antiquity, *"When lust has conceived, it brings forth sin"* (James 1:15). This is true for everybody, everywhere, in every generation, every culture, and all the time. There are no exceptions!

A bold German church leader named Deitrich Bonhoeffer lived and ministered during the dark days of Hitler's Nazi domination. Pastor Bonhoeffer penned a similar warning to those who would be leaders in the Kingdom of God (it was

73

published many years after his martyrdom in a Nazi prison in the book *Temptation*):

> In our members there is a slumbering inclination toward desire, which is both sudden and fierce. With irresistible power, desire seizes mastery of the flesh. All at once a secret, smoldering fire is kindled. The flesh burns and is in flames. It makes no difference whether it is a sexual desire, or ambition, or vanity, or desire for revenge, or love of fame and power, or greed for money . . . . At this moment God is quite unreal to us. He loses all reality, and only desire for the creature is real. The only reality is the devil. Satan does not here fill us with hatred for God, but with forgetfulness of God . . . . The lust thus aroused envelopes the mind and will of man in deepest darkness. The powers of clear discrimination and of decision are taken from us. It is here that everything in me rises up against the Word of God . . . . Therefore the Bible teaches us in times of temptation in the flesh, there is one command: FLEE! Flee fornication! Flee idolatry! Flee youthful lusts! There is no resistance to Satan in lust other than flight. Every struggle against lust in one's own strength is doomed to failure.[1]

The great danger with great power is great deception. King David followed the path to sin's door described perfectly by James the apostle more than one thousand years later, which is quoted in full below:

> But each one is tempted when, by his own evil desire, he is dragged away and enticed. Then, after desire has conceived, it gives birth to sin; and sin, when it is full-grown, gives birth to death (James 1:14–15, NIV).

The Greek word translated as "lust" or "desire" is *epithumea*. The root of the word, *thumea*, means generally "good feelings." It can apply to any emotion and activity producing emotion, such as sex, power, or even the act of worship! This word has been used in the phrases "sacrifice of praise" and to "pour oneself out" to God in worship. What really marks this word is what precedes the root, the Greek prefix *epi*. This is the operative part of this word, and it doesn't mean "in or into," but "on." So it refers to "great feeling" *onto* someone or some thing.

When this word is translated as lust or desire, it isn't talking about a person who wants relationship. A person who is lusting doesn't want *you*, he wants what is *yours*. He wants your body, your submission, your money, or your obedience as an "object." This is not relationship or even friendship—this is possession and conquering. The ultimate end of *epithumea* is not love, it is *rape!* And this is what was going on within David.

Drawn by desire and enticed by lust, David deceived himself into believing that the law of God somehow did not apply to him. God's Word never changes and it applies to all. In Leviticus 20:10, the law of Moses commanded that any man who "commits adultery with another man's wife" be put to death along with the woman involved (we have a greater covenant of grace with God through Jesus Christ today, but just imagine for a moment what a law like this would do to the spiraling problems we face with widespread adultery and a high divorce rate).

When David's unchecked desire led to sin, he became desperate to cover up his sin. Inevitably for *all* of us, lies devised to cover our sin only lead to *greater sin!*

When Bathsheba discovered she was pregnant and sent a secret message to King David, he devised an elaborate plan to fool her husband into sleeping with Bathsheba so that the child's true father would appear to be Uriah. The plot thickens and sickens at every turn. Although Uriah was a Hittite, he was also one of David's "Thirty Mighty Men." This man had proven his utter loyalty, courage, and character to David over many years and countless battles. He was part of David's elite inner circle of trusted warriors.

Driven by desperation and guided by a mind clouded in deception, David recalled Uriah from the battlefront on a false pretext and asked the loyal soldier, "How is Joab and *how goes the war*?" (2 Samuel 11:7). To David's dismay, Uriah refused to sleep with his wife, Bathsheba, out of *loyalty* to his troops.

> Uriah said to David, "The ark and Israel and Judah are staying in tents, and my master Joab and my lord's men are camped in the open fields. How could I go to my house to eat and drink and lie with my wife? As surely as you live, I will not do such a thing!" (2 Samuel 11:11, NIV).

Until this fateful spring, King David presumably had followed the same honorable warrior code. He belonged in the open fields, sleeping in a campaign tent. Once he followed his lust and stepped out of his proper position, he felt trapped in his sin.

Desperate to conceal his shameful act, David reverted to "plan B" with Uriah. He got him drunk and once again tried to get him to sleep with Bathsheba. Ironically, David was dealing with a loyal soldier that he had trained with meticulous detail. The David *who trained Uriah* would have done the same thing.

> At David's invitation, [Uriah] ate and drank with him, and David made him drunk. But in the evening Uriah went out to sleep on his mat among his master's servants; he did not go home (2 Samuel 11:13, NIV).

77

Some scholars believe the only reason Uriah did *not* spend the night with his wife was because he suspected the affair between his wife and King David. That is entirely possible—not all men are fools or unaware in affairs of the heart; only *some* of us are.

However, as one of David's Thirty Mighty Men, Uriah had already proven on the school of real life that he was absolutely loyal to his commander and king. David the warrior-king had also earned Uriah's loyalty in the life-and-death environment of mortal combat, and up until this fateful time in David's life, no one had any reason to suspect that David had changed his ways.

Many people today do not realize that the type of sacrificial leadership Uriah exhibited (in which a leader refused to enjoy pleasures his troops cannot enjoy) is *still* a respected leadership trait fostered in certain modern military organizations.[2]

Finally, King David wrote a letter to General Joab ordering him to *have Uriah killed* in battle. Then David adds insult to injury by sealing the message and sending Uriah himself to deliver his own death warrant to Joab. David knew that *Uriah was too honorable* to open the dispatch containing his own death warrant. In fact, David *counted on it.*

This Bible passage represents one of the cruelest illustrations of the seducing power of lust and sin in the human soul.

> In the morning David wrote a letter to Joab and sent it with Uriah. In it he

wrote, "Put Uriah in the front line where the fighting is fiercest. Then withdraw from him so he will be struck down and die" (2 Samuel 11:14–15, NIV).

Under the influence of deception, we see David the shepherd boy who regularly risked his life to save his father's sheep from lions and bears now coldly sacrifices his servant's life to save his tarnished reputation.

The Consequences of David's Calamity

Seven deadly consequences came upon David because of his sin, his concealment by deception, and the deadly measures he took attempting to hide his personal shame and avoid public blame.

First of all, David immediately became a slave to Joab's blackmail, a man not known for his mercy, consideration, or kindness. The moment Joab read David's letter, the king's future suddenly rested in the hands of one of his most dangerous and unpredictable adversaries. In a quote worthy of an old Mafia movie, it has been said that "*A secret shared by two people is not a secret unless one of them is dead.*" David was about to live out this proverb.

Joab didn't mind killing another man for David—he had already killed thousands. But as soon as he read the letter, it was as if he folded it neatly and secretly put it—and David—in his pocket. In a very real sense, that letter later cost

David the life of his eldest son, Absalom. And it *almost* cost him the life of Solomon. That letter lifted Joab, with all of his amoral schemes and disloyal motivations—to a place of preeminence. It essentially made Joab politically *invincible* because all he had to do was publish that letter and David was done in Israel!

Second, David was wracked by horrible waves of inner guilt. He recorded his unbearable inward pain for all to see in the Psalms. After beginning Psalm 32 with descriptions of how blessed it is to have your sins forgiven, covered, and not counted against you; David described from personal experience what it feels like *not* to be blessed, with sin pressing on your soul:

> When I kept silent,
>> my bones wasted away
>> through my groaning all day long.
>
> For day and night
>> your hand was heavy upon me;
>> my strength was sapped
>> as in the heat of summer (Psalms
>> 32:3–4, NIV).

Third, and perhaps most serious of all, David's actions displeased the Lord. According to the Bible record in 2 Samuel:

> When Uriah's wife heard that her husband was dead, she mourned for him. After the time of mourning was over,

David had her brought to his house, and she became his wife and bore him a son. But *the thing David had done displeased the LORD* (2 Samuel 11:26–27, NIV, emphasis mine).

Fourth, David's willing accomplice *told*. In one sense, Bathsheba had no choice because the evidence of her adultery was guaranteed to come into public view in due time. The law was clear—those who committed adultery were condemned to death. It is reasonable to believe that David had assured this beautiful married woman that he would shield their sin from others through his privileged office as king. On the other hand, it seems clear this woman was interested in seeing how far this thing could go. Perhaps it *was* her secret ticket to the king's palace. Again, the Bible reveals it all with total amazing transparency.

The woman conceived and *sent word* to David, saying, "I am pregnant" (2 Samuel 11:5, NIV, emphasis mine).

Fifth, the child born because of their secret sin *died* (2 Samuel 12:18). Nothing good came of it! But much evil *did* come from it.

Sixth, in the process of David's trying to hide his guilt and sin, he ordered the cold-blooded murder of one of his most loyal and trusted bodyguards and soldiers (see 2 Samuel 11:17). This was someone David knew in ways you can only expe-

81

rience by facing death together in the midst of continuous stress, hardship, and difficulty. When David added cruel murder and betrayal of a friend to his adultery, things went from bad to worse!

Finally, David's life and reign were *changed* forever. The king's rapid descent into such depths of sin and deception produced betrayal, murder, death to his own offspring, and a curse upon his family line that would only be redeemed through the death and resurrection of *the Son of David* about a thousand years later.[3]

David virtually became odious in the nostrils of Israel once the sordid truth of his lustful sin and murderous betrayal was published across the land. It wasn't something he could hide or make go away, and his people began to hate him just as they had hated Saul.

This is the sad story—and the *true story*—of David's darkest hour. When the *man after God's own heart* decides to become the *man after his own lusts*, he can unravel his own destiny and bring destruction on his family line in less than one day.

We should continually thank the Lord for the power of the Cross and for God's loving kindness and mercy.

Have you ever been at this place in your own life? Do you still cringe over unwanted memories of past mistakes and sins? Do you understand how you reached this place, and why?

Once you come into relationship with God in Christ, everything else that you get from God is paid for with the coin of commitment, discipline, and surrender.

Many people really don't have a proper understanding of salvation. They mistakenly believe that once they receive Jesus Christ and become Christians, then everything will work out automatically. Five or ten years go by and they find themselves contemplating divorce, battling addictions, or struggling with seemingly endless fears and physical symptoms related to those fears.

Please understand that the grace of God that saves you and brings you to Jesus is absolutely free. You can't earn it, you can't buy it, and you can't "deserve it."

However, once you come into relationship with God in Christ, everything else that you get from God is paid for with the coin of commitment, discipline, and surrender. That's incredible!

It looked like David's end—but, oh, what a God we serve! He is the God of forgiveness!

Notes

1. Dietrich Bonhoeffer, *Temptation* (New York: Macmillan, 1953), pp. 116–117.

2. For instance, a retired U. S. Marine Corps officer has confirmed to me that his military organization specifically trains its officers never to eat *before* their troops do. They are careful to put the welfare of their personnel above their own.

3. *Nelson's Bible Dictionary* approximates Samuel's death around 1,000 B.C. (see the article, "Samuel, Books of . . . ." in *Nelson's Illustrated Bible Dictionary* (Nashville, TN: Thomas Nelson Publishers, 1986).

CHAPTER 5

THOU ART THE MAN!

The Faithfulness of God in the Failure of Man

> *And David said to Nathan, I have sinned against the Lord. And Nathan said to David, the Lord also has put away your sin: you will not die.*

2 Samuel 12:13

This ancient testimony from the Book of 2 Samuel allows us to peer into the eternal stage for a preview of what Jesus Christ would accomplish on the Cross many generations later. After David offered humble and unconditional repentance, openly confessing his sin to the Lord, the Lord responded by *putting away David's* sin so that he would not die.[1] There is no greater passage or picture of *repentance* anywhere than this.

Perhaps you remember the prophetic announcement of John the Baptist to his disciples when Jesus appeared on the bank of the river Jordan: "Look, the Lamb of God, *who takes away the sin* of the world!" (John 1:29, NIV, emphasis mine).

Repentance seems to be the key that releases the Lord's supernatural removal of our sin. Unfortunately, we usually use *"repentance"* to describe our *sorrow* for sin or our *mourning* over past sin.

How many times have you looked at somebody with tears flowing down his cheeks and said, "Oh look, he is repenting and making things right with God." In reality, that might not be the case at all.

The basic meaning of repentance is not a matter of *feeling*. It is a matter of *will*.

The English word *repentance*, as it is commonly understood, *does not fully represent the biblical meaning*. We use repentance to describe our emotional feelings of sorrow or regret over *getting caught* or over *the consequences* of our actions. It isn't wrong to feel sorrow for either of these things, but it *isn't enough*.

Prisons around the globe house masses of men and women who have experienced genuine *sorrow* over getting caught committing crimes. Many who do not know the love of Jesus Christ continually mourn over the painful consequences their choices and actions brought into their lives; yet statistics indicate most of them will commit the same crimes again as soon as they are released into the general population!

Perhaps that is because most people think the basic meaning of repentance is a matter of *feeling*, but it is not. It is a matter of *will*.

True repentance is best understood not as a change of mood but as *"a change of mind."* Even better, think of repentance as *"a paradigm shift"* in value judgment.

One dictionary definition for *paradigm* is "a set of assumptions, concepts, values, and practices that constitutes a way of viewing reality for the community that shares them, especially in an intellectual discipline."[2]

In the apostle Paul's view, there are *two different kinds of sorrow*. He said, *"Godly sorrow brings repentance that leads to salvation* and leaves no regret, but *worldly sorrow brings death"* (2 Corinthians 7:10, NIV).

Of course *there is emotion* in repentance, but any emotions or feelings you experience should be understood as the *results* of true repentance, not its cause. Paul clearly separates *"godly sorrow"* from the *"sorrow of the world."* What he called the *"sorrow of the world"* is produced by the world of *circumstances*. It amounts to regret or emotional pain you feel because you "got caught" or suffered the pain of exposure. This worldly kind of sorrow isn't really concerned about the character of sin; it is mostly focused on its *consequences*.

The apostle literally said in the King James Version, "The godly sorrow *alone* works for salvation . . . ." This *"godly sorrow"* is true repentance.

True repentance puts the emphasis on turning *from* sin and to *Another*.

Paul is saying that this kind of sorrow towards God produces *"a change of mind—a paradigm shift—that never shifts or changes again."* On the other hand, the *"sorrow of the world"* produces only continual guilt, regret, and ultimate *death*.

Both John the Baptist and Jesus began their ministries crying *"Repent—change your mind!"* It is obvious that this kind of repentance will include grief or humiliation in many cases, but that is not the *primary* meaning or purpose of repentance.

True repentance puts the emphasis on turning *from* sin and to *Another*. We miss the point when we focus instead on the *emotion* occasioned by that desire or decision to stop sinning. You may be shocked to learn that *nowhere* in Scripture are we taught to measure or even value the *"amount of emotion" involved in repentance!* That means:

1. It *does not matter* whether guilt over sin is dealt with purely in a life-changing *resolve* to turn from sin to Christ, or accompanied as well by a river of *tears*.

2. Repentance is the *turning point* of salvation. It is a matter of your will, not of your feelings. Feelings may accompany your decision to turn

around, but feelings alone aren't enough to get the job done.

These principles occur often in King David's personal life and public ministry. Nowhere does God's Word say that David was a perfect man. In fact, the brutally honest confessions of David's sins and missteps as man and leader make it clear: he was totally human, he was flawed, and he was imperfect.

Yet God declared of this man who had (1) been consumed with lust, (2) committed adultery, (3) plotted a mass deception, and (4) ordered the cold-blooded murder of his own bodyguard and respected military leader to cover his sin: *"I have found David son of Jesse a man after my own heart; he will do everything I want him to do"* (Acts 13:22, NIV).

What was his secret? David loved God with all of his heart, and he lived for those moments of intimacy with God. When his sin separated him from his holy God, he openly and humbly repented. David had learned the power of true repentance and possessed the genuine resolve required to back it up. This released the grace of God to cover the weakness of his flesh.

All of this is expressed in the core text that launched this chapter: "And David said to Nathan, *I have sinned against the Lord. And Nathan said to David, the Lord also has put away your sin: you will not die"* (2 Samuel 12:13).

David's confession and God's forgiveness is a picture of the *faithfulness* of God in the *failure* of man.

By the time Nathan held this historic exchange with the king, David's most trusted (and most untrustworthy) general, Joab, had returned to Jerusalem from the Ammonite capital of Rabbah (the site of the modern city of Amman, the capital of Jordan). And he had carefully leaked word about *"Uriah's letter."*

There was another "leak" as well. The *messenger* whom Joab had dispatched to report Uriah's death to David was *also* emboldened to *"get his place in the sun."* He publicly gossiped about the king's hypocrisy and complicity in Uriah's murder.

Worst of all, it seemed that *Heaven* itself had closed its window of blessing. David's harp gathered cobwebs as his heart shriveled and the rivers of living water within dried up. We see the agony of David's heart revealed for those with discernment displayed in Psalm 32:

> When I kept silent,
>   my bones wasted away
>   through my groaning all day long.
>
> For day and night
>   your hand was heavy upon me;

my strength was sapped
as in the heat of summer (Psalm
32:3–4, NIV).

The apostle Paul described to the Ephesians
how the unchanging God responds to our sin and
to our repentance. His words also describe the
divine mercy displayed in David's life at the peak of
his sin and apparent disqualification. Paul wrote,
"But because of his great love for us, God, who is
rich in mercy, made us alive . . . ." (Ephesians 2:4–5a,
NIV).

When David sinned with Bathsheba and cruel-
ly engineered Uriah's death, Christ and the miracle
of the Cross were still future events according to
man's timeline. However, the *mercy of God* was
very much in operation on behalf of His children.

The prophet's job was to deliver what St. Augustine called "the severe mercy" of God.

Israel's brightest earthly light and most charismatic leader needed saving. A psalmist's divine
call needed salvaging. A wayward king at the
height of his form needed correction. The Lord's
response was to send in a gift from heaven in the
form of a humble prophet named Nathan. His job
was to deliver what St. Augustine called "the
severe mercy" of God.[3]

The unwelcome truth is that *all of us* need a God-given "*Nathan*" in our lives—people who love us enough to *tell us the truth* and stand by us in times of crisis can spare us a lifetime of sorrow, pain, and regret! Paul urged us to live with truth and love together, "... *speaking the truth in love,* we will in all things grow up into him who is the Head, that is, Christ" (Ephesians 4:15–16, NIV).

Even Paul had "*Nathans*" bringing encouragement in his life at critical moments. Perhaps the first was a prophet named Ananias, whom God sent to deliver a prophetic word to Saul of Tarsus (later called Paul), a man who was famous for his hatred of Christians and for his violent zeal in imprisoning them as chief agent of the Sanhedrin (see Acts 9 for the amazing story). Nathan faced the same fearful assignment: to take a message from God to a man possessing complete earthly authority to order his immediate imprisonment or execution.

Another time, God sent a "Nathan" named Titus to bring encouragement during a particularly dark season of Paul's life and ministry:

> For when we came into Macedonia, this body of ours had no rest, but we were harassed at every turn—conflicts on the outside, fears within. But God, who comforts the downcast, comforted us by the coming of *Titus* . . . (2 Corinthians 7:5–6, NIV, emphasis mine).

God May Send *You* a "Nathan" in a Time of Need

God did not fail David, even when David failed Him so miserably. Since God doesn't play favorites (He is "no respecter of persons" according to Romans 2:11), He won't fail to send *you* a "Nathan" in your time of need. Consider these promises God has made to those covered under His covenant love:

Jeremiah 32:40, NIV

"I will make an everlasting covenant with them: I will never stop doing good to them, and I will inspire them to fear me, so that they will never turn away from me."

Jeremiah 32:42, NIV

"This is what the LORD says: 'As I have brought all this great calamity on this people, so I will give them all the prosperity I have promised them.'"

Jeremiah 33:20–21, NIV

"This is what the LORD says: 'If you can break my covenant with the day and my covenant with the night, so that day and

night no longer come at their appointed
time, then my covenant with David my
servant—and my covenant with the
Levites who are priests ministering
before me—can be broken and David
will no longer have a descendant to reign
on his throne.'"

Job 14:16, NIV

Surely then you will count my steps
but not keep track of my sin.

What Was Nathan's Message to David?

Nathan had not spoken with David for seven
years, not since he had delivered the prophetic
word concerning the "house of the Lord" (see 2
Samuel 7:5–17), a word so precious to David that he
"hid [it] *in his heart that he might not sin against the
Lord"* (Psalm 119:11).

Unfortunately, David had conveniently forgotten or set aside God's warnings about adultery,
scheming against a neighbor, lying, and murder.
(*No one* can succeed by "selectively" hiding God's
Word in his heart.)Yet God still showed David
mercy by sending him Nathan with God's Word
and God's wisdom on how to deliver it.

Nathan placed his life in God's hands when he said to his king: "*Thou* art the man!"

First, Nathan the prophet spoke quietly and framed his case in a *parable*—in the same way that Jesus often spoke when He walked the earth.

Nathan *"brought a case"* before King David in the king's official capacity as the supreme judge in Israel. He was careful and wise to frame his case as a parable without specific names:

> "There were two men in a certain town, one rich and the other poor. The rich man had a very large number of sheep and cattle, but the poor man had nothing except one little ewe lamb he had bought. He raised it, and it grew up with him and his children. It shared his food, drank from his cup and even slept in his arms. It was like a daughter to him.
>
> "Now a traveler came to the rich man, but the rich man refrained from taking one of his own sheep or cattle to prepare a meal for the traveler who had come to him. Instead, he took the ewe lamb that belonged to the poor man and prepared it for the one who had come to him" (2 Samuel 12:1–4, NIV).

Second, David responded by immediately flying into a rage. Indignant and angry, the warrior-king shouted out loud:

> "As surely as the LORD lives, the man who did this deserves to die! He must pay for that lamb four times over, because he did such a thing and had no pity" (2 Samuel 12:5–6, NIV).

Once again, Israel's greatest king had accurately recalled and recited the Law of the Lord from Exodus 22:1 that requires a four-fold restoration for killing another man's livestock and because he "had no pity." Then David *oversteps* the Law by himself abandoning *pity* and condemning the man to death for his crime!

Third, Nathan looked into David's eyes and placed his life in God's hands when he said, "*Thou art the man!*" The prophet's quiet but God-inspired word pierced through the clouds of self-deception and confusion swirling around David. It hit David like the *stone* that brought down Goliath!

Clearly and sharply King David suddenly saw himself as the one "*who had no pity.*"

- He had exploited Bathsheba for *adultery.*
- He had *stolen* Uriah's home.
- He had murdered Uriah in *cold blood.*
- He had *implicated* Joab in his crime and empowered him for political blackmail.

- He had sinned against Abigail and the rest of his *family*.

- He had occasioned *blasphemy* against God Himself.

According to the sacred laws which he was sworn to uphold, *David deserved to die* for each of these capital offenses:

> If a man commits adultery with another man's wife—with the wife of his neighbor—both the adulterer and the adulteress must be put to death (Leviticus 20:10, NIV).

> If anyone takes the life of a human being, he must be put to death (Leviticus 24:17, NIV).

Sin Blinds and Then Binds Us!

How could such a lover of God, a hero through faith, and a psalmist of Israel, fall so low so quickly? The answer is that **sin blinds!** It blinds us to its presence in our lives, and then it **binds** us as slaves to its temporary thrills and the chilling fear of discovery.

- The *greedy* often preach and rail the loudest against "*Mammon-worship*."

- The *fornicator* is often the harshest on the *sexual sins of others.*

- The back-stabber and cruel *critic* is quickest to condemn others for *slander.*

- It is easy to count as self-virtue our denunciations of our own weaknesses seen in *others!*

No one understands sin better or describes it more accurately than Jesus. He understands the *deceitfulness of sin,* and He came some two thousand years ago to set our entire species free from its grip. It was Jesus who said, "Why do you look at the speck of sawdust in your brother's eye and pay no attention to the plank in your own eye?" (Matthew 7:3, NIV).

If you learn how to walk and live in "self-awareness" (not thinking "more highly" of yourself than you should according to Romans 12:3), then you will tend to deal sensitively with people who have fallen into sin or temptation. You will be willing to leave the final decision on their eternal reward to God, whose *"eyes are as a flame of fire"* (Revelation 2:18).

In David's case, God faithfully sent a gentle but accurate prophet to remove the beam from David's eye and end the blinding spell of the *"father of lies."*

Notes

1. God's forgiveness and the salvation we receive through Jesus Christ forever remove our eternal guilt in the eyes of God, but they do *not* deliver us from the *earthly consequences* of our choices in this life. The Lord often moves to untangle our lives or even deliver us from many of those consequences, but these are "extra" acts of divine mercy and grace. The man on death row who genuinely repents of his sin is instantly forgiven and made a new creature in Christ, no matter how heinous his crimes. However, his sentence to earthly death delivered by an earthly court is not automatically set aside—he simply comes to death's door and passes into God's presence as a sinner saved by grace. The thief who repents and is saved must still return his stolen goods and pay whatever earthly price comes because of his actions. The Scriptures also teach us he must retrain his hands, habits, and thinking patterns to do honest work instead of resorting to theft (see Ephesians 4:28).

2. Definition for "paradigm" from Dictionary.com. *The American Heritage® Dictionary of the English Language,* 4th ed. Houghton Mifflin Company, 2004. Accessed: August 11, 2008 at http://dictionary.reference.com/browse/paradigm.

3. The term "a severe mercy" may be traced to *The Confessions of St. Augustine.* While I do not necessarily agree with all of the writings or views of St. Augustine, his writings contain certain insights of great value to Christians from many different backgrounds. In *Confessions*, this ancient church leader described how pain and suffering led him to receive the saving grace of God in this passage: *"And thou, O Lord, didst press upon me in my inmost heart with a severe mercy, redoubling the lashes of fear and shame; lest I should again give way and that same slender remaining tie not be broken off, but recover strength and enchain me yet more securely."*

I do not say the Lord uses fear and shame for His purposes, but He *does* cause all things to "work together for good" (Romans 8:28). I see God's "severe mercy" in Jesus' prophetic warning to Peter: "Simon, Simon, behold, Satan hath desired to have you, that he may sift you as wheat: But I have prayed for thee, that thy faith fail not: and when thou art converted, strengthen thy brethren" (Luke 22:31–32). Satan brought the sifting and the Lord Jesus supplied intercessory prayer and deliverance, bringing Peter new strength through trial. In "severe mercy," the Lord uses the consequences of our pride and stubbornness (or the enemy's attacks) for salvation, deliverance, character development, and ultimate good.

CHAPTER 6

REPENTANCE: THE TURNING POINT OF SALVATION

David's Repentance

"If ever a word from human lips fell with crushing weight, and with the illuminating power of a flash of lightening, it was this. The judgment blared like a trumpet in the inmost soul of the king, making him tremble."

—F. W. Krummacher[1]

David suddenly saw himself not as a judge and lawgiver, but as law-breaker, a guilty *criminal* who was much more worthy of death than the fictitious sheep thief he just condemned to death.

In spite of his profound respect and love for David—indeed *because* of it—Nathan the prophet now moved past his personal "point of no return" to clinch the point and accuse the king of murder.

101

His purpose wasn't merely to condemn, but to point his royal hearer to "the turning point of salvation."

With each word and phrase, the prophet opened himself to the risk and real possibility that royal anger would flare and a quick death sentence would follow.

> "This is what the LORD, the God of Israel, says: 'I anointed you king over Israel, and I delivered you from the hand of Saul. I gave your master's house to you, and your master's wives into your arms. I gave you the house of Israel and Judah. And if all this had been too little, I would have given you even more. Why did you despise the word of the LORD by doing what is evil in his eyes? You struck down Uriah the Hittite with the sword and took his wife to be your own. You killed him with the sword of the Ammonites. Now, therefore, the sword will never depart from your house, because you despised me and took the wife of Uriah the Hittite to be your own.'
>
> "This is what the LORD says: 'Out of your own household I am going to bring calamity upon you. Before your very eyes I will take your wives and give them to one who is close to you, and he will lie with your wives in broad daylight. You did it in secret, but I will do this thing in broad daylight before all Israel'" (2 Samuel 12:7b–12, NIV).

David recorded his *response* for us in Psalm 51. His words of humble repentance have been repeated in tearful prayer by untold millions of Christian and Jewish people over the centuries. When we experience repentance and hunger for forgiveness that seem to overpower any words available to us, we turn to this gem of godly repentance and supplication in the ancient Psalms:

> Have mercy upon me, O God, according to thy loving kindness [*hesed*]: according unto the multitude of thy tender mercies blot out my transgressions.
>
> Wash me thoroughly from mine iniquity and cleanse me from my sin (Psalm 51:1–2).

This confession, if sincere and true, *always* receives a quick response from our merciful Father. The Bible record in 2 Samuel 12 assures us that after David offered this prayer of repentance, he was heard, received and *cleansed* of his sin:

> And David said unto Nathan, I have sinned against the LORD. And Nathan said unto David, The LORD also hath put away thy sin; thou shalt not die (2 Samuel 12:13).

Whatever a man sows, that he will also reap.

Galatians 6:7, NKJV

This principle dates back to the beginning of time and human existence in the Garden of Eden, and perhaps even further. It seems that a certain anointed cherub whose duty was to cover Almighty God with worship and praise was the first to discover this divine principle.

When Lucifer violated his holy trust and conspired against his Creator, he reaped an eternal whirlwind of sorrow. He moved in sly deduction in the Garden to draw the human race into his failed rebellion and eternal separation.

Thank God for Jesus Christ who restored us to fellowship! Once we are restored to God's family through faith in Jesus, we come under the Father's love *and* His loving correction once more. The Bible says:

> My son, do not make light of the Lord's discipline, and do not lose heart when he rebukes you, because the Lord disciplines those he loves, and he punishes everyone he accepts as a son (Hebrews 12:5–6, NIV).[2]

Many of us seem to be confused about divine forgiveness and the natural consequences of our choices in life. One of the old adages passed down from the past in the world says, "What goes around *comes* around."

As Christians, we should always go to God's Word for the *final word* on how to deal with sin.

What does God do when we *first* turn to Him

from a life of sin and folly through Jesus Christ? God says:

- He will have compassion on us.
- He will tread our sins underfoot.
- He will hurl our iniquities (lawless ways) into the depths of the sea (see Micah 7:19, NIV).
- He won't treat us as our sins deserve.
- He won't repay us according to our iniquities (lawlessness).
- He will love us with a love as great as the height of the heavens above the earth.
- He will remove our transgressions from us as far as the east is from the west (see Psalm 103:10–12, NIV).

What happens when we betray His love and trust after we become Christians, when we have walked with God in intimate communion and spiritual ministry? **Sin must be *purged* and *purified* from our souls by whatever *"means of grace"* God chooses.**

Ever since Jesus paid the supreme price for our sin on the Cross, our sins have been covered by His blood. His innocence covers and removes the eternal punishment for our guilt. This is the grace of God in operation.

The soul must have a mind change, a brain washing, a change in its thinking and decision-making process.

However, we all possess a *soul*—the place of our minds, our will, and our emotions. It is here that must have a mind change, a brain washing, a change in our thinking and decision-making process. This is where the "purging and purifying" process must take place. Otherwise, we will return to our sin again and again while foolishly assuming God will pardon our presumption "right up to the pearly gates."

David cried out to the Lord in his great psalm of repentance:

> Cleanse me with hyssop, and I will be
> clean
> wash me, and I will be whiter than snow
> (Psalm 51:7, NIV).

Part 1: The Consequences of Murder

King David's life displays how we must often endure the soul-cleansing properties of consequences even though we receive God's instant forgiveness for our sins. In verses 10–11 of 2 Samuel 12, we see how the purging from God answers to the sin of man. These verses speak directly to David's *murder* of Uriah, an innocent man. The prophet declared the prophecy of "the sword" on God's behalf:

> "You struck down Uriah the Hittite with the sword and took his wife to be your own. You killed him with the sword of the Ammonites. Now, therefore, *the sword will never depart from your house*, because you despised me and took the wife of Uriah the Hittite to be your own" (2 Samuel 12:9–10, NIV, emphasis mine).

There were *three* awful fulfillments of this "prophecy of the sword" in David's family line. All of them linked directly with the consequences of David's decision to sin before the Lord. While David's sin was forgiven immediately after he repented before the Lord, the earthly consequences his sin set in motion would follow him throughout his life and even beyond the grave.

The first fulfillment occurred in 2 Samuel 13:28 with *the murder of Amnon, David's firstborn son,* by Absalom, his *favorite* son.

Amnon succumbed to lust and brutally violated his half-sister Tamar. Then he abandoned her in her shame, even though Tamar told him and begged him to marry her in a proper way. When David failed to do anything to bring about justice, Tamar's eldest brother Absalom, secretly plotted revenge. Two years later he masterminded Amnon's murder:

> Absalom ordered his men, "Listen! When Amnon is in high spirits from drinking wine and I say to you, 'Strike Amnon down,' then kill him. Don't be afraid. Have not I given you this order? Be strong and brave." So Absalom's men did to Amnon what Absalom had ordered. Then all the king's sons got up, mounted their mules and fled (2 Samuel 13:28-29, NIV).

The *second* fulfillment of the prophecy came about years later with *the murder of Absalom* by Joab, David's commander-in-chief of the army and cousin! The murder took place in direct violation of David's personal order, right in front of the king's two other generals!

> Joab said, "I'm not going to wait like this for you." So he took three javelins in his hand and plunged them into Absalom's heart while Absalom was still alive in the oak tree (2 Samuel 18:14-15, NIV).

The sword struck David's family the *third* time soon after his death when King Solomon ordered the execution of Adonijah, David's second son (by a different woman than Bathsheba).[3]

Part 2: The Consequences of Adultery

The second half of Nathan's prophecy to King David dealt with the severe earthly *consequences of adultery*. Immediately after the prophet described the judgment of "the sword" in David's family for his act of premeditated murder, Nathan launched into a second penalty area centered upon the king's shameless adulterous affair.

> "This is what the LORD says: 'Out of your own household I am going to bring calamity upon you. Before your very eyes I will take your wives and give them to one who is close to you, and he will lie with your wives in broad daylight. You did it in secret, but I will do this thing in broad daylight before all Israel'" (2 Samuel 12:11–12, NIV).

There are *two* parts to the fulfillment of this prophecy. Again, remember that David received immediate forgiveness for his trespass against God, but the consequences are serious and painful for any leader who forsakes his or her responsibilities as a model and leader in the name of the Lord.

God canceled the written decree of death that David really deserved under the Law of Moses—the same law the rest of Israel was expected to live by. The Lord granted David forgiveness and a reprieve from death because of the king's genuine repentance, because of His own grace and compassion, and because of His promise to David and his Seed.

The Lord delivered His decree of forgiveness and pardon quickly through Nathan's spoken prophecy, *"Thou shalt not die!"* (see 2 Samuel 12:13b), but the trail of sorrow was about to begin. Long after the sounds of the retreating prophet's final footsteps had faded from the king's quarters, David lingered in a time of stillness to incarnate and understand all that had happened. That stillness was disturbed by the frightening cry of Bathsheba's *baby*. Instantly the prophet's final words burned into David's mind and soul, for Nathan had seen this coming by the Spirit and prophesied it.

> Nathan replied, "The LORD has taken away your sin. You are not going to die. But because by doing this you have made the enemies of the LORD show utter contempt, *the son born to you will die"* (2 Samuel 12:13–14, NIV, emphasis mine).

The Bible describes David's agony in painful detail, as he fasted and begged God to *spare* his son. But he had already doomed his son by his choices.[4]

> David pleaded with God for the child. He fasted and went into his house and spent the nights lying on the ground. The elders of his household stood beside him to get him up from the ground, but he refused, and he would not eat any food with them (2 Samuel 12:16–17, NIV).

The agony David experienced over his *own* sin is hauntingly similar to the agony the "Son of David" endured over the sins of the world. Sin *always* brings pain and sorrow, whether it comes sooner or later.

King David agonized over the suffering his *own* unrighteousness caused his newborn son. King Jesus, whom Malachi called "the sun of righteousness,"[5] would also agonize over the suffering He would have to endure because of *our sin*. This holy Son of God who was totally without sin literally *became* sin and paid the supreme price to take away *our* sin forever![6]

Even in the midst of King David's darkest sin, we see hints of God's great act of selfless love for a selfish world. Generations later, One called the Son of David pulled back the veil and declared the mystery of God's great love: "For God so loved the world, that he gave his only begotten Son, that whosoever believeth in him should not perish, but have everlasting life" (John 3:16).

As painful as the first fulfillment of this prophecy was, a second fulfillment was yet to come. The consequences of David's sexual sin brought even more sorrow through the blatant sins of David's favorite son, *Absalom*. Nathan the prophet declared in advance exactly what would happen:

> "'. . . because you despised me and took the wife of Uriah the Hittite to be your own.'

111

"This is what the LORD says: 'Out of your own household I am going to bring calamity upon you. Before your very eyes I will take your wives and give them to one who is close to you, and he will lie with your wives in broad daylight. You did it in secret, but I will do this thing in broad daylight before all Israel'" (2 Samuel 12:10b–12, NIV).

Years later Absalom brought Nathan's prophecy to pass with chilling accuracy and bitter cruelty, bringing shame on himself, on his father's house, and on his nation. And it all came about through the counsel of one who was fancied as Israel's wisest counselor to kings:

> Ahithophel answered, "Lie with your father's concubines whom he left to take care of the palace. Then all Israel will hear that you have made yourself a stench in your father's nostrils, and the hands of everyone with you will be strengthened." So they pitched a tent for Absalom on the roof, and he lay with his father's concubines in the sight of all Israel (2 Samuel 16:21–22, NIV).

David's two-fold sin (involving adultery and premeditated murder) was *purged* as he remained faithful to God—even as the Lord's strange and painful *"means of grace"* to cleanse his soul was worked out. This two-fold purging process lasted more than twenty years.

David Repents and Worships Again

"And David said unto Nathan, 'I have sinned against the LORD.'"

King David rose again because he willingly bowed down in repentance *first*. When Nathan confronted David with his sin, the king offered no excuses, explanations, or justifications. He immediately confessed that he had *sinned* against the Lord.

(Notice that he didn't do what most of us do and say, "I've made a *mistake*." Most of the time, there is no "mistake" involved unless you consider "getting caught" to be a mistake.)

After his child died, David arose, cleaned up, anointed himself with ointment, changed his attire, and went at once to the tabernacle. In other words, David again became a true *worshiper* of God.

Have you ever thought about the necessary elements of "true worship"? True worship is not just emotional singing, praising, or dancing. It includes at least three things that we see throughout the Bible, whether in the Old or the New Testament:

1. *Acknowledge* God as God of all.

2. *Accept* God's way without debate.

3. *Approve* of all God does, no matter how sad or difficult it is.

113

After David turned his life over to God in this way, his wife Bathsheba conceived again and gave birth to another son, Solomon—*"the peaceable one"* (*Shelomah*—a variation of Shalom). Solomon's birth brought another message from Nathan the prophet, a wonderful prophecy:

> David comforted Bathsheba his wife, and went to her and lay with her; and she bore a son, and she called his name Solomon. And the Lord loved [the child];
>
> He sent [a message] by the hand of Nathan the prophet, and [Nathan] called the boy's [special] name *Jedidiah* [*beloved of the Lord*], because the Lord [loved the child] (2 Samuel 12:24-25, AMP, italics mine).

As you study and think about David's dark night of the soul, remember that the Lord's prophecies concerning David and his seed were still waiting for fulfillment. The birth of David's second child through Bathsheba marked the birth of a "child of promise," through whom God would fulfill His promises to David.

It was for this reason that He sent Nathan the prophet to declare a "special name" over Solomon: *"Jedidiah,"* the *"Beloved of the Lord"* or better, *"Because Jehovah loves"* (Unger). This was God's way of bringing *laughter* back to David's heart.

What a fitting conclusion to this heart-wrenching saga! This is the mercy and grace of God

114

etched in the life of the Sweet Psalmist of Israel! It is the "breadth, length, depth, and height" of God's love that Paul struggled to describe in Ephesians 3:18–19, previewed in advance of Calvary in "living color" in David's life.

Step back from this story mentally and try to grasp "how much" God loved David (and *still loves you* at this very moment). He had brought David from being:

- An **adulterer**
- A **murderer**
- A **hypocrite**
- A **liar**
- **Broken**
- **Defeated**

. . . to being a man who was:

- **Forgiven**
- **Purged**
- **Sanctified**
- **Fit for the Master's** use once again!

This is our hope and assurance when we trust in the faithfulness of God in the failure of man. It is proof positive of the promise, "For it is God who works in you to will and to act according to his

115

good purpose" (Philippians 2:13, NIV).

When you live by faith in the faithfulness and unconditional love of God, then you can trust (with David before you) that the prophetic destiny of your life has every hope of *fulfillment*—even in your failures. This is the mercy and grace of our God in full operation!

> Or do you show contempt for *the riches of his kindness, tolerance and patience,* not realizing that *God's kindness* leads you toward *repentance*? (Romans 2:4, NIV, italics mine).

> But *because of his great love for us,* God, who is rich in mercy, made us alive with Christ *even when we were dead in transgressions*—it is by grace you have been saved. And God raised us up with Christ and seated us with him in the heavenly realms in Christ Jesus (Ephesians 2:3–6, NIV, italics mine).

Notes

1. F. W. Krummacher, *David, King of Israel.* Trans. M. G. Easton (Grand Rapids, MI: Kregel Classics, 1994). (Originally published by T&T Clark, Edinburgh), p. 295.

2. This New Testament passage is a quote from Proverbs 3:11–12.

3. See 1 Kings 2:25.

4. Had the child lived he would have been a bastard saddled with unbearable shame and rejection all his life. At that time in Israel, an illegitimate child in Israel could not claim a paternal inheritance or demand to be treated as a member of the *family*. (Ironically, this was probably David's own lot as the illegitimate son of Jesse!) We know this much—whether the child lived or died, the sins of his father David had crippled the child's life.

   Most born-again Christians stand firmly against the "choice" of voluntary abortion, calling it instead by its true name: murder. We also clearly differentiate between illegitimate parents who conceive a child out of wedlock, and the child itself. There is no such thing as an "illegitimate child" in God's eyes. I believe David, with his probable illegitimate beginnings, is living proof of God's heart toward those "called by name while they are yet in their mother's womb" (see Isaiah 49:1).

   Ultimately, we must commit the complex case of Bathsheba's first child by David into the hands of our all-knowing and just God. However, we know that God is "no respecter of persons" (Acts 10:34). If God cared for Abraham's son by Hagar, although He knew

117

Ishmael's descendants would ultimately bring unthinkable sorrow and trouble to Abraham's descendants through Isaac; then we know that same God (who changes *not*) also took care of David's innocent offspring conceived in illegitimate lust.

For reasons unknown to us, circumstances sometimes cause certain people of widely varying ages to pass through premature physical death before experiencing eternal life, much as Lazarus passed through physical death before he experienced physical and spiritual resurrection for the "first time" under Jesus miracle ministry.

5. See Malachi 4:2.

6. Second Corinthians 5:21 says, "God made him who had no sin to be sin for us, so that in him we might become the righteousness of God."

CHAPTER 7

OFFENSE!

THE BIRTH OF THE ABSALOM SPIRIT

(2 Samuel 13–18)

Many times you can discover the strengths and weaknesses of leaders by examining their interactions with the *other* people in their lives.

The world learned more about Great Britain's royal family through the life and death of the late Princess Diana than the family ever wanted to reveal. The true depth of character in Mother Teresa was revealed not by the rich and powerful individuals who knew her, but by the untold thousands of utterly forsaken, broken, and destitute people she loved, clothed, fed, and comforted—even as many of them entered death's door.

One man illuminates David's extremely human weaknesses more than any other in this king's storied life. Absalom's role in his father's legacy was so important that the Holy Spirit devoted six chapters to his tragic life!

What vital lessons does Absalom's life contain for leaders in God's kingdom? His life frames one spiritual principle that we must understand above all:

Abused, misused or mismanaged ANOINTING will destroy the one who carries it!

Absalom was one of six sons born to David while he was king of Judah and based in Hebron. It is clear that this royal son had a marvelous anointing. Unfortunately, he would also become history's classic picture of an individual who was *destroyed by his own anointing!* He was undone by his own charisma, through his own extraordinary gifts.

Imagine the pilot of a fully loaded Boeing 747 airliner "going to sleep at the wheel" as the plane screams toward the earth for a disastrous landing. Blockbuster movies have been made portraying the drama when the captain of a nuclear attack submarine decides independently to go over "to the other side" or to launch a nuclear strike.

On a simpler and even more personal level, the idea of a drunk driver clumsily directing tons of steel toward innocent loved ones can strike terror in the calmest of hearts.

This is why we focus on Absalom. There is a vital balance between a person's character and his

120

or her gifts or anointing. This is especially true for anyone who feels called to the five-fold ministry (see Ephesians 4), or to leadership in society, commerce, or government.

All of us are made up or composed of a "gifts cluster." While no one is "good at everything," most if not all of us tend to be good or gifted in *some* things. Success and deep satisfaction in life seem to be centered in our ability to find our calling and focus on it with all of our ability and character.

The apostle Paul named a "gifts cluster" of five key gifts in Ephesians that Jesus has given the Church as "building" or construction and perfection gifts. He said Jesus ". . . gave some to be apostles, some to be prophets, some to be evangelists, and some to be pastors and teachers, to prepare God's people for works of service, so that the body of Christ may be built up" (Ephesians 4:11–12, NIV).

- *Apostles* are fathers and generals. They like to oversee things, govern things.

- *Teachers* explain the preaching and acts of apostles and prophets.

- *Prophets* clarify. They see things others don't and make them clear.

- *Evangelists* multiply. They are the only ones in the "five-fold gifts" that do not focus on church growth by addition, but rather by exponential multiplication.

• *Pastors* are, of course, the shepherds. They are the long-term caregivers who patiently tend the flock of God as under-shepherds of the Lord's crown jewel, the Church.

Since the body of Christ is still imperfect and in great need of being built up, it should be obvious that all five gifts are still needed and are still being given to the Church. This five-segment cluster mirrors the ancient Hebrew concept of the "*yad*" of God—the hand or the scepter of His power. The Lord said, "I have engraved you on the palms [*yad*] of my hands . . ." (Isaiah 49:16, NIV). He was saying in part, "You are an extension of My hand . . . ."

Some people erroneously believe a person operates in one of these *doma* (or "building/construction") gifts *exclusively* or not at all. It has been my experience that God imparts portions of all of these gifts in differing measure to each anointed leader He plants in the Church. Most tend to favor one gift over the others, with the other gifts arising in different measure as well.

In my life, for instance, I've discovered a clear gifts cluster emerging over the years. My first and most dominant gift is the function of apostle, then of teacher, and finally of pastor. My life and ministry demonstrate significantly lesser anointings of the evangelist and prophet.

These leadership gifts clusters don't seem to be limited to operations solely within the Body of

Christ. There are Christian leaders who appear to function as Christ-centered apostles of real estate, for instance. There are teachers and pastors operating to the glory of God in virtually every realm of legitimate human society and endeavor. These people are gifts of God planted in the kingdoms of man to establish and reveal the Kingdom of God in their midst.

This leads us to the main point of this chapter:

When you operate or function *outside* of the calling God has given you, things tend to go terribly wrong!

Anytime you try to operate outside of your "core" gifting, you won't be operating at your greatest efficiency and ability. It is important to find, develop and center upon the primary gifting God has given you.

A second truth is that when you focus on your gifts and abilities *but discard godly character and obedience to God*, your life can become a ticking time bomb moving relentlessly toward a frightening end.

As we noted earlier, Absalom was one of *six* sons born to David in Hebron—Amnon, Chileab, Absalom, Adonijah, Shephatiah, and Ithream (see 2 Samuel 3:2). We know nothing of Chileab (it is presumed that he died in infancy), but we *do* know that

Absalom killed his half-brother, Amnon, for violating his full-blood sister, Tamar (see 2 Samuel 13).

David had *many* children, but they were born to many different mothers. Each of these offspring claimed King David as father while clinging to personal loyalties to his or her individual mother. This also included their respective families, ethnic or national group, and culture.

Effectively, Absalom stepped into the place of David's *firstborn* heir to the throne when he arranged the murder of David's oldest son. The king seemingly always knew Absalom was the most gifted of all of his offspring.

Absalom was the only son of King David who was *royalty on both sides*. Absalom's mother, Macaah, was the daughter of King Talmai of Geshur. This princess bride gave birth to Absalom and Tamar as David's wife.

Geshur was a small, independent kingdom adjacent to Israel. This independent sovereignty came in handy after Absalom directed the assassination of Amnon. He simply crossed into his grandfather's kingdom and claimed refuge from Jewish law and David's soldiers.

Absalom was a remarkably *charismatic* young man. He was a "born leader" who liked to be followed, watched, and honored. There are at least seven reasons or pieces of evidence that he was uniquely positioned to captivate hearts in Israel.

    1. He moved to Jerusalem, the *capital city*

of the newly unified nation, early in life with his father.

2. He grew up in the king's *palace*, thoroughly exposed to power and politics.

3. He was David's *favorite* son.

4. He was also a favorite of the *people*.

5. He was charming, personally *attractive*, and unfortunately, he had the ability and the will to ingratiate[1] himself with people.

6. He also loved pomp and royal *pretense*— he provided for himself fifty men to run before his chariot.

7. His long, black hair was a sign of his special *favor*, his anointing, and of his pride; much like Joseph's coat of many colors. It would later betray him and become the primary instrument of his undoing.

One of the most important "reality checks" a Christian can experience is this: life is rarely simple, and the "reasons" for a person's descent into sin or failure are *never* totally "black and white." For instance, it is a fact that Absalom had *good reason* to **hate** his father.

Today we see David as "a man after God's own heart," but he was also a flawed man who sinned terribly while pursuing a perfect and loving God. The sins of a father can't *help* but cause serious

125

problems in his sons and daughters—especially if they are reinforced numerous poor decisions in his life.

Absalom had *good reason* to hate his father, David

King David's first reaction when he learned that Amnon had raped Tamar seemed natural and expected. He was angry (see 2 Samuel 13:21). But everything stopped there.

Absolutely nothing happened beyond David's passing show of anger. Those nearby must have felt as if they were watching an actor deliver the required emotion before walking off stage. Sadly, David's actions made it clear he felt no further responsibility to "live out" the script of a righteous father and king executing justice and protecting a victim.

Tamar may have been "only one of many" daughters born to David, but she was Absalom's *only* sibling. He was enraged that his sister was violated, but it is logical to assume he would have allowed justice to handle the problem if justice had ever been offered! The problem was that David— the victim's father, the family's patriarch, and Israel's chief lawgiver and sovereign king—essentially washed his hands of the affair and did *nothing* about it!

This is why Absalom felt he had good reason to hate his father. David's unwillingness to step in to right this wrong revealed his lack of concern about women. This must have doubled Absalom's fury over Tamar's humiliation and violation. He came to hate and disrespect David, but his anger quickly took a cold, cruel and calculating turn. Absalom waited and planned for the right time while Amnon continued on with what he thought would be a long life. Just two years later wily Absalom took matters into his own hands.

The Rise of the Absalom Spirit

In a real sense, David created this "Rebel Spirit" through his own *insensitivity* and failure! The respected scholar F. B. Meyer believed that Absalom's fratricide (brother-murder) would never have taken place if David had taken instant measures to punish Amnon.[2]

How often do you and I do this as *leaders*? You can count on it at virtually every level of leadership: **unresolved conflict produces** *the Absalom Spirit!*

Some say that David became ill and was pre-occupied with a disease at this time. In other words, it was the *disease* of the Bathsheba *adultery*.

Many of the Psalms written by David are literally his transparent prayer journal, a supernatural window into his intimate walk with our invisible God. When you read these words from Psalm 41, it is easy to see David's anguish over sin and the physical impact of it all that confined him to bed.

127

The LORD will sustain him on his
sickbed and restore him from his bed
of illness.
I said, "O LORD, have mercy on me;
heal me, for I have sinned against
you."
My enemies say of me in malice,
"When will he die and his name
perish?" (Psalm 41:3–5, NIV).

The man we see revealed in Psalm 55 is a person wracked by deep, perhaps even clinical,
depression, shadowed by a haunting death wish at
times. As we shall see, this perfectly matches with
some of David's bizarre actions during the
"Absalom years."

My heart is in anguish within me;
the terrors of death assail me.
Fear and trembling have beset me;
horror has overwhelmed me.
I said, "Oh, that I had the wings of a dove!
I would fly away and be at rest—
"I would flee far away
and stay in the desert;
Selah
"I would hurry to my place of shelter,
far from the tempest and storm."
(Psalm 55:4–8, NIV)

It is clear that David was suffering from a broken heart during those dark years. This chilling

narrative prayer should make us even more aware of how strategic Satan can be when stalking and plotting the downfall of a godly person. We have nothing to fear if we are "hiding in Christ," but we must be vigilant and on the alert.

During this dark four-year period of David's life, he seemed to waste away and was unable to do anything, while Absalom *undermined* his father and stole away the hearts of many of the people. Finally, when Absalom's rebellion reached its pinnacle and he established his kingdom in *Hebron* and was proclaimed king (although David was still alive and God's chosen vessel), it was evident that the people had lost their reverence and love for David.

For his part, King David recognized this as God's fiery *purging* of his own heart for his sins with Bathsheba and Uriah. Absalom saw things differently. To his jaded mind, David's dark night of the soul presented the ideal opportunity for him to get *revenge* upon the father he had come to hate!

The very anointing of Absalom to rule and lead was what ultimately *destroyed* him.

Absalom's bitter hatred for his father was the root of his own destruction, and it birthed the ungodly desire to *destroy* David and take his throne from him. This rebellious son was about to

129

become the "poster child" for this spiritual principle: "When bitterness gives rise to ungodly ambition in the heart of an anointed leader, it will always end in disgrace!"

This is the classic biblical case of the abuse, misuse and mismanagement of *anointing*! Why? It is because Absalom *used* his anointing to attempt to destroy his spiritual father!

If character and integrity are not the *keepers of the anointing*, then the anointing will break through and destroy everything it touches.

The anointing of God:
- births the force of *purpose* . . .

- brings the focus of *power* . . .

- builds the fire of *persistence*!

However . . .

If the ANOINTING is not harnessed by character and bridled by integrity, it can *destroy* as effectively as it can *build* the kingdom!

Many Christians in the Body of Christ today find themselves in this very predicament!

- *Full* of anointing . . . *and* brimming with bitterness!

- They misuse and abuse their anointing to *avenge* their bitterness!

- Inevitably, they *destroy* everything they touch—including their own marriage, children and reputation!

This is not a pretty picture! Absalom literally was destroyed by his own *anointing*! It seems clear that Absalom had the *greatest* anointing among all of David's sons. Unfortunately, he felt he had good reason to *hate* his father David. Because his *bitterness* was stronger than his *character*, Absalom ultimately destroyed his family, his followers and even himself!

Generations later, Peter addressed this brand of bitterness in Simon the Magician saying, "I perceive that thou art in the *gall of bitterness,* and in the *bond of iniquity*" (Acts 8:23).

The anointing is no match for *bitterness* in the human soul. Only godly *character* can drain the dregs of bitterness out of us. What do you do to steer clear of such a deadly soul disease? Be sure *your* anointing is harnessed by *character* and bridled by *integrity*!

PERSONAL APPLICATION

- How are *you* managing your anointing?

- Do you realize the very source of your

131

greatness in ministry can *destroy* as well as build the Kingdom?

- Have you seen evidence that abused, misused or mismanaged anointing will *destroy* the one who carries it?

- Are you certain that *"the keepers of the anointing,"* **character** and **integrity**, have harnessed and bridled your anointing so that it will build and establish and not destroy and ruin everything it touches?

Notes

1. *The American Heritage Dictionary of the English Language*, 4th ed. (Boston: Houghton Mifflin Company, 2003), s.v. *Ingratiate*: "To bring (oneself, for example) into the favor or good graces of another, especially by deliberate effort: She quickly sought to ingratiate herself with the new administration."

2. F. B. Meyer, *David: Shepherd, Psalmist, King*, p. 201.

CHAPTER 8

THE ABSALOM SPIRIT: UNFORGIVENESS AND ITS DEADLY CONSEQUENCES

(2 Samuel 15:1–12)

No action, whether foul or fair,
Is ever done, but it leaves somewhere
A record written by fingers ghostly,
As a blessing or a curse and mostly
In the greater weakness or greater
strength
Of the acts which follow it.

Henry Wadsworth Longfellow (1807–1882)

Long ago, God established a principle of order in our lives that helps us learn spiritual truths from created things. The Bible says, "The spiritual did not come first, but the natural, and after that the spiritual" (1 Corinthians 15:46–47, NIV).

We learn at an early age that a stone tossed into a body of water such as a pond or a lake causes a

133

disruption. Rippling continues to spread outward in ever-broadening circles. This principle takes a devastating form when deep-sea volcanic eruptions or earthquakes trigger gigantic tidal waves or "tsunamis." These waves may travel thousands of miles before crashing inland with waves standing ten to twenty-five feet above sea level.

Sin *always* disrupts human life. And it always tends to spread outward to affect others in its path, sometimes hundreds of years away in the time-line of human existence. Perhaps this is why it is said, "Forgiven men may have to reap the harvest they have sown."

Although God forgives men and women, that sin must be *purged* at every appearing to eliminate its deadly effect.

David's adultery opened the door for disaster to crash on the shores of his life. His affair with Bathsheba was more than a "passing romantic fling" (as modern social and entertainment commentators might call it). There is no such thing as "passing sin." Sin, at any level, disrupts human life. As F. B. Meyer said, "Sin may be forgiven, as David's was, yet a long train of sad consequences follow."

When David seduced Bathsheba and arranged the cruel death of her noble husband Uriah, he disrupted life for himself, for Bathsheba, for his nation, and for his future offspring. Yes, David repented and found forgiveness and personal restoration to God; yet two things remained that forgiveness would not remove.

An Immediate and Painful Consequence

The first consequence of David's sin was immediate and painful. David's child born to Bathsheba died in infancy. For seven days David fasted and prayed and lay on the ground. It seems he suffered more in that loss than if he himself had died. Bathsheba suffered as well. Can you imagine what pain her mother's heart endured watching her only child suffer and die—the innocent for the guilty?

The second consequence kicked in immediately, but it would linger in its power and effect for the rest of David's life. The king's open confession of guilt did not satisfy the critics who were away from God. No, in fact, *it provoked them to mockery and scorn* of David and his rule.

Why? Only the blood of the guilty can atone for such sin *in the eyes of those who do not know God's grace.* To speak of the *"Blood of the Lamb"* as one's substitute sacrifice is foreign to them. The unredeemed soul cries out for "an eye for an eye," and "a tooth for a tooth."

Mercy is a foreign concept, and grace is beyond human comprehension to the lost soul. Only vengeance will do, especially vengeance upon someone who in some way claims to live by a higher standard of morality, or who seems to walk "closer" to God than the lost soul does.

All we need to illustrate this point is the example of an internationally known evangelist's national exposure on videotape as the alleged client of a prostitute—after he criticized another televangelist on national television over accusations of sexual and financial impropriety. Mercy was hard to find in our nation (or in most churches) after the media blitz that followed.

Former *President Bill Clinton* suffered a great loss of prestige and leadership effectiveness when his sexual activities with a young female assistant were documented in lurid detail on national television. Whether one views it as fair or unfair, this story became the dominant legacy in the nation and around the world marking President Bill Clinton's two four-year terms in the White House.

The Absalom Spirit Sprang from David's Weakness as a Father

One of David's most serious and costly flaws was his apparent inability or unwillingness to *discipline* his own house. In the words of F. B. Meyer, "A man never sees the worst of himself until it reappears in his child."

According to the laws and customs of the day, the people thought King David should drown Tamar and destroy Amnon for his act of incest.[1] The king did neither.

Then, after Absalom openly engineered the murder of Amnon, again David failed to act. The people believed that David's weakness in not genuinely punishing Absalom's murderous act of revenge *disqualified* him as a leader-king.

When David finally commanded that Absalom be captured, he fled to Talmai, King of Geshur— his *grandfather* on his mother's side. Talmai "hid" Absalom for three years essentially *"in plain sight."* F. B. Meyer said, "How could David allot the penalty [for] his *son's* impurity *which he had evaded for himself?"* David's *pardon* of Absalom seemed to be "the last straw" in the eyes of his weary citizens and vocal critics. This indulgent father's heart was clearly conflicted, and the Scriptures confirm it.

And the soul of King David longed to go forth unto Absalom: for he was comforted concerning Amnon, seeing he was dead (2 Samuel 13:39).

Wily Joab the opportunist saw all of this unfold, and with uncanny skill he moved with stealth to take advantage of David's predicament—for his own *selfish* purposes as usual. Those purposes included his need to protect himself from complicity in Uriah's murder. He saw a way to do that neatly by arranging the pardon and reconciliation of Absalom with his father, the king.

Second, Joab wanted to secure his own position just in case Absalom might succeed to the throne. Joab was as dangerous in the political battlefield as he was at the warfront. This was never as clear as in this crisis.

The sophistication and skullduggery of Joab's scheme reveals the kind of man David had placed in his number two position of leadership. Joab arranged to hire a so-called *"wise woman"* to approach David. Don't be fooled by the Old English phrase used here. This was no "wise" woman; this was an "artful" and "cunning" woman.[2] She was essentially a professional *actress* or con woman from Tekoah.

After she heard Joab's proposal, this woman agreed to pretend to be a widow before King David, claiming she had two sons who had fought until one of the sons died (see 2 Samuel 14:2–3). She came before the king, fell on her face and asked for help. She told David her entire family wanted to kill her sole living son, leaving her childless.

The Bible says David was moved to compassion and said: "As the Lord lives, there shall not one hair of thy son's head fall to the ground" (2 Samuel 14:11b). As soon as she heard the king's compassionate assurances, she set the "hook" exactly as wily Joab had coached her to do.

The pretender cautiously pointed out to David that he would be guilty of sin against God if he did not call his own son back from exile. After delivering a message of moral preaching to the king mixed with liberal amounts of sly flattery and fawning humility, David finally smelled a rat. He commanded the woman to tell him the truth and then asked, *"Is not the hand of Joab with thee in all this?"*

Snared in Joab's Trap

He was snared in Joab's trap, even as Joab stood there during the "wise" woman's Emmy-award winning performance. But he knew he was caught, and the bait so closely resembled what he *wanted* to do anyway, that he willingly slipped his head through Joab's political noose.

King David agreed to pardon Absalom and gave Joab permission to bring him home. For all these reasons and more, many in Israel felt David was no longer *worthy* to be king. The man who had vanquished powerful enemies and armies in battle after battle was suddenly seen as weak, indecisive, immoral in heart, and prone to give preferential treatment to his own (after all, he exempted himself, Bathsheba, and now his sons—first Amnon, then Absalom—from the laws of God).

A majority of David's subjects in Israel and Judah now openly despised him and loathed his government. This set the stage for the *"Gethsemane"* of David's life and reign.

Absalom's Rebellion

Professional communicators and educators like to say, "You cannot *NOT* communicate." I know that statement might sound confusing at first, but it makes more and more sense the longer you think about it. Whether you are shouting from the rooftop or "stonewalling" a friend or spouse with the "silent treatment," you *are* communicating. "No answer" is actually a very clear answer.

139

The same truth applies to your actions. Your actions really *do* speak louder than words most of the time. And virtually every great "rebel" in the Bible and in *our* lives has left a tell-tale trail of clues about how they were transformed from lawful to lawless leaders. They basically *prepared themselves* for failure.

How did Absalom prepare for revolt?

Absalom's first and greatest step toward failure was his refusal to forgive his father, David, for his failure to discipline Amnon. He refused to embrace forgiveness and chose instead to nurse his anger for years.

Paul the apostle warned us, "Don't let the sun go down while you are still angry, for anger gives a *mighty foothold* to the Devil" (Ephesians 4:26–27, NLT). The King James Version calls it "giving place" to the Devil. The original Greek word used here, *topos*, refers literally to property or real estate. It seems that Absalom's choice to cling to anger toward his father essentially gave Satan *legal right of access and use* to part of his soul.

David continued to contribute to Absalom's preparation for rebellion as well. When David refused to see Absalom for two more years as a *humiliation* to him, it drove Absalom's *hatred* of David to a new, deeper level.

Unfortunately, anger is a state of mind and soul that quickly leads to action. With the fires of anger fueling his emotions and contaminating his spirit, Absalom began immediately to lay the groundwork for his rebellion.

He yielded to his consuming ambition and desire for admiration from the people by seizing princely *authority* and position in the realm. He publicly took on the habits of kings and conquerors when he hired fifty horsemen, horses and carriages to go before him in public.

It is interesting that the Lord specifically warned us *not* to put our trust or affections in the strength of war horses and chariots in the Psalms: "Some trust in chariots, and some in horses: but we will remember the name of the LORD our God" (Psalm 20:7).

Absalom also "played to the common people" with pomp and ceremony. With a "trademark" move now associated directly with his name, Israel's crown prince schemed and connived to seize by craft what would have been his by relationship—and without any additional effort on his part!

(This should remind us of Satan's successful attempt in the third chapter of Genesis to talk Adam and Eve into eating the forbidden fruit to "grasp" the "God-likeness" they *had already been given freely* by God!)

Absalom was especially skilled at currying the *favor* of the vast crowds of Israelites from out of town who came to the capital seeking justice in King David's busy palace.

His "if only" speech was particularly effective:

> He would get up early and stand by the side of the road leading to the city gate. Whenever anyone came with a complaint

to be placed before the king for a decision, Absalom would call out to him, "What town are you from?" He would answer, "Your servant is from one of the tribes of Israel." Then Absalom would say to him, "Look, your claims are valid and proper, but there is no representative of the king to hear you." And Absalom would add, *"If only I were appointed judge in the land! Then everyone who has a complaint or case could come to me and I would see that he gets justice."*

Also, whenever anyone approached him to bow down before him, Absalom would reach out his hand, take hold of him and kiss him. Absalom behaved in this way toward all the Israelites who came to the king asking for justice, and so he stole the hearts of the men of Israel (2 Samuel 15:2–6, NIV, emphasis mine).

Absalom simply searched out and identified those in leadership who were most likely to join in a *rebellion* against authority. Virtually everyone interested in or duped into sowing discontent in a local church or region follows in these footsteps of Absalom. This is especially true of leaders who are highly placed or who are related to the chief leader in some way.

David's dark night of the soul was marked by one of the greatest betrayals of the Old Testament. It happened when Absalom won the loyalty of

King David's most trusted and respected counselor, a man named Ahithophel (or "brother of folly").[3]

Ahithophel's keen insights and wise counsel won such acclaim that "the advice of Ahithophel, which he gave in those days, was as *if one had inquired at the oracle of God*" (2 Samuel 16:23, NKJV).

His son, Eliam, was one of King David's bodyguards; and this son had a *daughter* named Bathsheba.[4] Many scholars suspect Ahithophel held a secret offense toward David because of his sin against and with Bathsheba, his granddaughter.

Exactly forty years after Samuel anointed David at Bethlehem and four years after Absalom returned from Geshur, the crown prince launched his plot to overthrow his father. It began with a request to David for a royal blessing on Absalom's plan to journey to Hebron to fulfill a vow to God made during his stay (or rebellious self-exile) in Geshur (see 2 Samuel 15:8).

Absalom sent spies throughout Israel to seek out willing partners in the rebellion plot and to organize them. His spies said to each new recruit, *"As soon as you hear the sound of the trumpets, then say, 'Absalom is king in Hebron'"* (2 Samuel 15:10, NIV, emphasis mine).

When Ahithophel received Absalom's personal summons, he cast aside years of service to King David and immediately joined Absalom's political coup (v. 12). The betrayal broke King David's heart. It also reveals to us just how powerful Absalom had become, because Ahithophel didn't have a track record for choosing losing sides.

The Revolt Unleashed

When the time was right and Absalom's anger was at its peak, the revolt within his heart unleashed a revolt that swept through Israel in a tidal wave of popular sentiment.

Absalom's act of betrayal coupled with Ahithopel's uncanny counsel instantly up-ended Israel's government in a bloodless coup.

Absalom was in, David was out. The son-who-would-be-king entered Jerusalem triumphantly with counselor, royal chariot, and his usual fifty runners. Meanwhile, David—the Sweet Psalmist of Israel—quietly escaped under cover of night with a small band of discouraged and heartbroken supporters. Both the famous father and his rebellious son provide proof for the statement:

"Everything you do strengthens or weakens everything else you do."

Several things happened *immediately* after Absalom launched his revolt. The *first* thing was a polarization of the land that showed up in several ways. Absalom chose Hebron (the capital of Judah) as his capital city—retracing the footsteps of his father. His choice also highlighted and increased the perceived competition and strain between Israel and Judah. It was a decision designed to confuse and complicate loyalties in

Israel, since Hebron was the burial place of the Patriarchs.

The enemies of David seemed to come out of the underbrush—just like snakes that they were. If you function as a leader in God's kingdom at any level, then understand that *there are always Ahithophels*—even in the most peaceful organization! It seems apparent that Ahithophel hated David for his sin with Bathsheba, his granddaughter.

While you're looking out for challenges and opposition, you are about to meet two other men in the next section who seem to appear in every century and virtually every organization in some form or another. *Don't forget them: Shimei and Ziba.*

We will also meet the loyal friends and supporters of David who also stepped up to the plate—God always has heroes in waiting to support the people who do His will, even in their darkest hour.

David's Response to Absalom's Revolt

A messenger came and told David, "The hearts of the men of Israel are with Absalom."

Then David said to all his officials who were with him in Jerusalem, *"Come! We must flee, or none of us will escape from Absalom. We must leave immediately, or he will move quickly to overtake us and bring*

145

ruin upon us and put the city to the sword" (2
Samuel 15:13–14, NIV, emphasis mine).

As you read this Bible passage, did it occur to
you that David's response seems *out of character* for
such a great warrior of God? King David was not
concerned with *his own safety* in physical combat.
The only issue that mattered was the safety of
Jerusalem, *the city* God loved so much, and the
safety of his *people.*

David faced a crucial *spiritual* conflict within
the sanctuary of his own soul:

- Would he surrender to God and
  allow the Most High to resolve this
  revolution and restore peace to
  Jerusalem and Israel, or . . .

- Would he take matters into his own
  hands and "fight back"?

This is the true *core* and *cause* of every conflict
in the life and ministry of a true man or woman of
God! **The Enemy is not them; it is always Him!** In
this battle, *the winner always loses* and *the loser
always wins!*

David understood this truth. The late W.
Phillip Keller, celebrated best-selling author of *A
Shepherd Looks at Psalm 23* and *David, the Shepherd
King,* said of this quality in David, *"It was the vein
of pure gold in his conglomerate character."*[5] In other
words, David *would pay any price to make things
right with God!*

The desperate flight from Jerusalem marked David's second darkest hour, his *public* Gethsemane. Nearly everything of value in his life seemed to be shaken.

- His own son sought to kill him.

- His people turned from him.

- His military prowess was denied to him by God.

- Nathan's prophecy came to pass in public view, exactly as predicted in Second Samuel 12:7–14 (especially verse 11):

"This is what the LORD says: 'Out of your own household I am going to bring calamity upon you. Before your very eyes I will take your wives and give them to one who is close to you, and he will lie with your wives in broad daylight'" (2 Samuel 12:11, NIV).

David *knew* that all this was God's personal *purging* and divine discipline for him. When Nathan the prophet confronted David with his sin, his response was instant, direct, and clear of any excuses or self-justification: *"And David said unto Nathan, I have sinned against the LORD. And Nathan said unto David, The LORD also hath put away thy sin; thou shalt not die"* (2 Samuel 12:13).

The New Testament echoes the great virtue of

147

such heartfelt repentance in response to God's loving rebuke and correction in the Letter to the Hebrews:

And ye have forgotten the exhortation which speaketh unto you as unto children, My son, despise not thou the chastening of the Lord, nor faint when thou art rebuked of him: For whom the Lord loveth he chasteneth, and scourgeth every son whom he receiveth. If ye endure chastening, God dealeth with you as with sons; for what son is he whom the father chasteneth not? (Hebrews 12:5–7).

David was truly repentant. F. W. Krummacher said David was "prepared from the heart to submit to all the consequences of his sin." Asaph the Psalmist put words to David's sorrow over sin's effect on his relationship with God when he said, *"Whom have I in heaven but Thee? There is none upon earth that I desire beside Thee"* (Psalm 73:25).

This was David's hardest battle to lose! He wrote in the Twenty-seventh Psalm, "Take everything if You must, O Lord, but do not withdraw Your face from me; do not leave me away from Your grace!" (Psalm 27:9).[6]

Notes

1. F. W. Krummacher, *David, King of Israel*. Grand Rapids: Kregel, 1994, p. 313.

2. *Biblesoft's New Exhaustive Strong's Numbers and Concordance with Expanded Greek-Hebrew Dictionary* (copyright © 1994, 2003 Biblesoft, Inc. and International Bible Translators, Inc.), s.v. "wise," OT:2450, *chakam* (khaw-kawm'); Hebrew from OT:2449; wise, (i.e. intelligent, skilful or artful): KJV - cunning (man), subtil, ([un-]), wise ([hearted], man).

3. *Biblesoft's New Exhaustive Strong's.* s.v. "Ahithophel," OT:302, 'Achiythophel (akh-ee-tho'-fel); Hebrew from OT:251 and OT:8602; brother of folly; Ahithophel, an Israelite.

4. See 2 Samuel 23:24, 11:3, respectively.

5. W. Phillip Keller, *David, the Shepherd King, Volume 2* (Waco, Texas: Word Books, 1996), p. 125.

6. Author's summary of this verse.

CHAPTER 9

FRIENDS AND ENEMIES AT THE CRISIS POINT

Picture David the giant killer, the hero of Israel, the sweet psalmist and redeemer of his people, *fleeing for his life* from military death squads released by his own ambitious son! Now picture the King of Kings, the only begotten Son of God, the world's only sinless man, being pursued like a criminal by His own creation.

It is often said that no parent should have to outlive his or her children. Let it also be said that no parents should have to flee the murderous plots of their own children. This kind of heart-wrenching parallel between the life of David and the sacrificial life of Jesus (called "the Son of David") becomes a dominant theme during David's dark night of the soul.

The Bible paints a portrait of the sorrow, desperation, and incredible pain David suffered during Absalom's rebellion. It also demonstrates the behavior of true friends and true enemies "at the midnight hour" of our lives.

A Sorrowful Crossing of the Kidron Valley

- **King David**

  The whole countryside wept aloud as all the people passed by. *The king also crossed the Kidron Valley, and all the people moved on toward the desert* (2 Samuel 15:23, NIV).

- **The Lord Jesus Christ** (after His "high priestly prayer" and before His Gethsemane experience)

  When he had finished praying, *Jesus left with his disciples and crossed the Kidron Valley.* On the other side there was *an olive grove,* and he and his disciples went into it (John 18:1, NIV).

Tears over Jerusalem, Surrender to God

- **King David**

  And David went up by the ascent of *mount Olivet,* and *wept as he went up,* and had his head covered, and he went barefoot [the sign of a slave]: and all the people that was with him covered every man his head, and they went up, weeping as they went up . . .

And it came to pass, that when David was come to the top of the mount, where he *worshiped* [**shachan**—"to prostrate oneself before God"] . . . (2 Samuel 15:30, 32; emphasis mine).

"If I find favor in the LORD's eyes, he will bring me back and let me see it and his dwelling place again. But if he says, 'I am not pleased with you,' then *I am ready; let him do to me whatever seems good to him"* (2 Samuel 15:25–26, NIV, emphasis mine).

• **The Lord Jesus Christ**

When he came near the place *where the road goes down the Mount of Olives,* the whole crowd of disciples began joyfully to praise God . . .

. . . As he approached Jerusalem and saw the city, he *wept over it* (Luke 19:37a, 41; NIV, emphasis mine).

Jesus went out as usual to the Mount of Olives . . . knelt down and prayed, "Father, if you are willing, take this cup from me; *yet not my will, but yours be done"* (Luke 22:39, 41b–42, NIV, emphasis mine).

153

Some Stayed Behind, Some Accompanied Them

- **King David** left ten concubines at the palace and was accompanied by mighty men.

The king set out, with his entire household following him; but *he left ten concubines to take care of the palace* (2 Samuel 15:16, NIV).

. . . all the people and *all the mighty men* were on his right hand and on his left (2 Samuel 16:6b, emphasis mine).

- **The Lord Jesus Christ** left nine behind and took three for company

Then Jesus went with his disciples to a place called Gethsemane, and he said to them, *"Sit here while I go over there and pray."* He took Peter and the two sons of Zebedee *along with him,* and he began to be sorrowful and troubled (Matthew 26:36–37, NIV, emphasis mine).

These life parallels between David and the Lord Jesus, as with most biblical parallels, should not be taken too far. For instance, the events that occurred with David's concubines cannot be linked or compared with the events that followed in the lives and ministry of the nine disciples of Jesus. The apparent link is simply that some were left behind and some came along.

However, these examples *do* illustrate the remarkable foreshadowing of the Messiah's life and ministry in David's life more than a thousand years earlier.[1]

Most important of all we see the roles played by God-given friends in times of crisis; and the sadly predictable roles of enemies and those who misunderstand God's leaders in those same difficult times.

Friends at the Midnight Hour

Samuel Taylor Coleridge said, *"Friendship is a sheltering tree."* Thank God for every *true* friend He sends into your life.

Genuine friends shelter us from the withering heat of criticism and the chilling effect of rejection. They warm us with their unconditional love and cool us with wise counsel in times of stress and aggravation. Their mere presence reflects the presence and comfort of God in times of loss and despair, and a friend's unflagging support encourages us to reach higher and go farther than we could ever dream on our own!

It has been said that you can measure a person's value by the longevity and quality of their friendships. David had some genuine friends. Many of them had stood with him since the dark days of exile in the cave Adullam. Others who arrived to stand with him in the Absalom crisis were new friends—and a good number of them were "foreigners" who felt drawn to David by God. Each of them was a gift of God to an anointed servant facing a dark night of the soul.

- **Ittai the Gittite**

    This friend was actually a Philistine who brought with him six hundred horsemen simply to serve King David! At first, David thought Ittai was merely defecting to Israel from Achish of Gath, the King of the Philistines. He actually tried to release Ittai to remain in Jerusalem to serve whoever emerged victorious. David discovered that Ittai did not come to join the "winning organization." He came to join the "true king."

    But Ittai replied to the king, "As surely as the LORD lives, and as my lord the king lives, *wherever my lord the king may be, whether it means life or death, there will your servant be*" (2 Samuel 15:21, NIV, emphasis mine).

    This level of loyalty and God-inspired faithfulness pays off. David would later promote Ittai the Gittite (the Philistine) to commander of one-third of his army!

- **Zadok and Abiathar**

    These leading priests helped King David bring the Ark of the Covenant to Jerusalem shortly after Israel crowned him king. The men watched and listened as David made his great confession of faith and commitment on his *second* attempt to bring the Ark of the Covenant to Jerusalem. (His errors and lack of knowledge in the first attempt ultimately cost the life of a priest and discouraged the nation as described in 2 Samuel 6).

    This is the declaration David made before the Lord, long before the final outcome of his second attempt was known:

Then the king said to *Zadok*, "Take the ark of God back into the city. If I find favor in the LORD's eyes, he will bring me back and let me see it and his dwelling place again. But if he says, 'I am not pleased with you,' then I am ready; let him do to me whatever *seems good to him*" (2 Samuel 15:25–26, NIV, emphasis mine).

157

At King David's request, *Zadok* and *Abiathar* returned to Jerusalem and served as priests *under Absalom's rule* and became *spies* for David. Their sons, Ahimaaz and Jonathan, also served David as trusted *messengers* and risked their lives relaying vital information between the priests and the king in exile.

• **Hushai the Archite**

And it came to pass, that when David was come to the top of the mount, where he worshiped God, behold, Hushai the Archite came to meet him with his coat rent, and earth upon his head (2 Samuel 15:32).

Hushai the Archite was one of King David's top two counselors. However, Hushai was much more than a royal counselor. According to 1 Chronicles 27:33, "Ahithophel was the king's counselor: and Hushai the Archite was *the king's companion* [*reyah*—'friend']."

This is the true friend who met weary King David at the high point of a mountain and at the second-lowest point of his life. This was David's surprising response:

David said to him, "If you go on with me, then *you will become a burden* to me. But *if you return* to the city, and *say to Absalom,* 'I will be your servant, O king; as I was your father's servant previously, so I will now also be your servant,' then *you may defeat the counsel of Ahithophel* for me" (2 Samuel 15:33–34, NKJV, emphasis mine).

Was King David telling his friend, "If you insist on going with me, you will be a *drag, a pain, a dead weight"*? The Hebrew word translated as "burden" is *massa*. In this passage, it really means:

- "a burden lifter"
- "an oracle of God"
- "a joy and comfort"

That means David was *understood* to be saying, "Hushai, I would *love* to have your comfort, wisdom and solace in my time of suffering." That becomes clear when David asks his friend for perhaps the greatest (and most dangerous) favor of his life.

The king asked Hushai to return to Absalom's illegal government as a *double agent* to defeat the dangerous counsel of wise Ahithophel. *So Hushai became, in effect, David's "angel of comfort" in his darkest hour.* Once again, we see a foreshadowing of a far greater angel of comfort appear to console and strengthen another king greater than David.

159

[Jesus] withdrew about a stone's throw beyond them [in Gethsemane], knelt down and prayed, "Father, if you are willing, take this cup from me; yet not my will, but yours be done." *An angel from heaven appeared to him and strengthened him* (Luke 22:41–44, NIV, emphasis mine).

Hushai kept David informed of Absalom's plans directly from the enemy's inner counsel. You, too, have a "planted source" who can hear and relay the slightest detail of your enemy's plans. The Holy Spirit functions as our "angel of comfort," but He is *more* than an angel, and as God, He is omnipresent. He can reveal every plan the enemy (Satan or his agents) makes against us. No one is better able to thwart the *"wiles of the Devil"* commissioned against us.

All you need do is stay in close communication with Him. Just remember that the Omnipresent Spirit who dwells in your heart simultaneously overhears *every scrap* of counsel in the chambers of Hell. Because he knows all things, there are no *secrets* He does not know.

Nothing in all creation *is hidden from God's sight*. Everything is *uncovered and laid bare before the eyes of him* to whom we must give account (Hebrews 4:13, NIV, emphasis mine).

Enemies at the Midnight Hour

Just as your friends will seem to come out of the woodwork in your Gethsemane season, so will your *enemies*. David had three old enemies who came to work their ways at this painful and vulnerable time in his life.

- **Ziba—the greedy opportunist (2 Samuel 16:1–4)**

  David had appointed Ziba to manage the estate of Mephibosheth, the last living son of his deceased friend, Jonathan (and Saul's last descendant). Ziba and his fifteen sons and twenty servants were responsible for tending the flocks, tilling the fields, and keeping Jonathan's son rich and well-cared for. The *New Living Translation* describes Ziba's duties clearly:

  Then the king summoned Saul's servant Ziba and said, "I have given your master's grandson everything that belonged to Saul and his family. You and your sons and servants are to farm the land for him to produce food for your master's household. But Mephibosheth, your master's grandson, will eat here at my table." (Ziba had fifteen sons and twenty servants.)

Ziba replied, "Yes, my lord the king; I am your servant, and I will do all that you have commanded." And from that time on, Mephibosheth ate regularly at David's table, like one of the king's own sons.

Mephibosheth had a young son named Mica. From then on, all the members of Ziba's household were Mephibosheth's servants. (2 Samuel 9:9–12, NLT).

> While Ziba seemed to say the right thing and show up with food and supplies at certain prominent moments, the "abundance of his heart" managed to betray in slandering words what was really in his heart. David would learn in the end that Ziba was an opportunist and exploiter.

1. Ziba provided needed food and drink while David and his royal party were on the run from Absalom's forces. When King David noticed that Mephibosheth was missing and asked about Saul's grandson, **Ziba lied,** saying, "[Mephibosheth] is staying in Jerusalem, because he thinks, 'Today the house of Israel will give me back my grandfather's kingdom'" (2 Samuel 16:3, NIV).

2. This lie caught David off-guard. He believed for a moment that Mephibosheth

betrayed his grace. Based on that lie, David said in essence, "Okay, then *you can have Mephibosheth's estate!*" (see 2 Samuel 16:4).

3. The *true story* emerged in the end when Mephibosheth showed up with the "rest of the story," revealing yet **another lie by Ziba.** The servant had disobeyed lame Mephibosheth's request that he saddle a donkey for him so he could join David. Then Ziba left him behind in Jerusalem without a word, and put words into Mephibosheth's mouth to misrepresent him to David (see 2 Samuel 19:26–30).

- **Shimei—misplaced offense (2 Samuel 16:5–14)**

  After David started down the other side of the Mount of Olives in his desperate flight from Jerusalem, he came to a narrow valley. Shimei, a distant relative of Saul, suddenly appeared on a ridge above them and began to curse David and throw stones at him.

As he cursed, Shimei said, "Get out, get out, *you man of blood*, you scoundrel! The LORD has repaid you for all the blood you shed in the household of Saul, in whose place you have reigned. The

163

LORD has handed the kingdom over to your son Absalom. *You have come to ruin because you are a man of blood!"* (2 Samuel 16:7–8, NIV, emphasis mine).

All of Shimei's accusations were incorrect and misplaced. However, David knew that God was using Shimei to draw out *one more accusation against him* stemming from his original sins with Bathsheba and Uriah. In other words, David considered Shimei's outrageous insults to be just another part of his purging.

When Abishai and Joab, David's military leaders, wanted to kill Shimei, David said, *"It may be that the LORD will see my distress and repay me with good for the cursing I am receiving today"* (2 Samuel 16:12, NIV). David just let it go! (At least for the time being.)

- **Ahithophel—"the gall of bitterness" (2 Samuel 16:20–17:23)**

    As we noted earlier, Ahithophel quickly switched sides and joined Absalom as *"chief counselor"* on Absalom's first day in Jerusalem. Keep in mind that he was Bathsheba's *grandfather*, and he *never* forgave David for his relationship with her.

Ahithophel's first word of counsel to Absalom was that Absalom *have sexual relations with David's ten concubines* (secondary wives in the royal harem), *and that he do it in public!* (See 2 Samuel 16:20–23.) In all probability, there were at least three reasons for this heinous advice:

1. Nathan *prophesied* it would happen as a part of David's punishment in 2 Samuel 12:11–12 (NIV):

"This is what the LORD says: 'Out of your own household I am going to bring calamity upon you. Before your very eyes I will take your wives and give them to one who is close to you, and he will lie with your wives in broad daylight. You did it in secret, but I will do this thing in broad daylight before all Israel.'"

2. This act would make reconciliation impossible between Absalom and David! And that offered "benefits" to both Absalom (his men will know that he was *"his own man"*) and to Ahithophel (if David could not forgive Absalom again, then it would become an "insurance policy" against David becoming king again and ordering Ahithophel's execution as a traitor).

3. Perhaps most important to Ahithophel: *Absalom's public rape of his father's wives* would provide exquisite Middle Eastern-style "eye for an eye, tooth for a tooth" *revenge* for David's sexual seduction of his granddaughter, Bathsheba, and the loss of face it represented to her family.

However, Ahithophel's cunning work was not yet complete. He offered Absalom yet another word of counsel with potentially deadly consequences to King David (see 2 Samuel 17:1–4):

- Send an army of twelve thousand men after David *immediately*, *"this night."*

- Catch David while he is weary and weak. Threaten his followers so they will abandon David.

- Then *kill David only*, and swing the *loyalty* of the people back to Absalom with a promise of immunity.

This advice pleased Absalom and the elders with him. *It should have!* It was brilliant in every respect. In fact, it would have eliminated David as a threat once and for all. The good news is that God already had a plan, and David, even at such a low ebb in his life as God's leader, had put the plan into effect.

Before making his decision on Ahithophel's advice, Absalom called in Israel's "second-greatest counselor" for advice—*Hushai* the Archite.

We don't really know whether Absalom called for a second opinion because of *political considerations* or to seek counsel from someone with *military experience*. What we *do* know is that God was using Hushai to preserve the "man after His own heart." Hushai's counsel is recorded for all time in 2 Samuel 17:7–14.

- *You will not get David if you follow Ahithophel's advice.*

- He is too smart and experienced to camp with his troops.

- You will be accused of slaughter if you kill other Israelites besides David with your *"Special Forces hit team!"*

- Take a huge army of volunteers from Dan to Beersheba and *personally lead them yourself* into battle.

- Have this army of Israelites from every tribe kill David and all his men so that only *one* story is told of the battle. This will *implicate* every tribe in David's execution.

- If a city takes David in, destroy it completely so that no *witnesses* are left.

167

The elders preferred Hushai's counsel over Ahithophel's, perhaps because it was more brutal and gory. In that instant, Ahithophel saw that he was finished. He got his affairs in order, went home, and hanged himself (see 2 Samuel 17:23).

Almost immediately, Hushai and King David's priestly spy network got word back to the king so that he quickly led his army out of Israel's territory to safety. (See 2 Samuel 17:21–22.)

Absalom could not (or *chose not to*) forgive an old offense by his father, King David. His choice *not to forgive* literally destroyed his and David's peace. What a destructive thing *unforgiveness* is!

The *root of bitterness* grows inside your soul if not dug out by the spade of repentance! And when bitterness flowers as it did with Elymas the Sorcerer (Acts 13:8) and with Absalom, it destroys all it touches! Do not carry unforgiveness in your heart for even sixty seconds longer! The unwillingness to forgive contaminates. Bitterness kills.

Notes

1. David's birth is placed at B.C. 1083 by *McClintock and Strong Encyclopedia, Electronic Database.* Copyright © 2000, 2003 by Biblesoft, Inc. All rights reserved.

CHAPTER 10

THE JOAB SPIRIT: THE SPIRIT OF DISLOYALTY AND BETRAYAL

(1 Kings 2:1–6)

Nearly every four years in the U.S. presidential term cycle, headlines hit magazine stands and the talking heads on Internet and electronic news media outlets alert us to yet another *"insider exposé."* The source always seems to be some highly placed but deeply dissatisfied White House staffer.

Most of these people claim their former bosses were unethical, ruthless, unfair, or outright foolish and unlawful in their conduct of presidential affairs. Nearly all of these authors are tainted with an obvious credibility problem: If the revelation they share is so dire and unlawful, then *why did they wait so long to reveal it?*

The answer usually isn't hard to find—there is significant profit to be made by dishing dirt on any American president, and often there is a *revenge factor* at work.

The same thing happens in virtually every other relatively free nation. For instance, the royal family in the United Kingdom deals constantly with exposé books, magazine articles, and press conferences claiming to have "the inside scoop" on the ruling family.

Sometimes genuine wrongs must come to light and blatant, willful sins must be exposed (as in Nathan's confrontation of David, and in some of the modern-day scandals in a few prominent American ministries). In reality, God is well able to bring hidden things to light.

Anyone who has lived more than three decades will tell you these "hidden" things usually surface despite the best efforts of leaders to stop them, simply because of the vast number of people required to run a large government or church ministry—people who *must* be included in the inner circle of information flow and the decision-making processes of leadership.

On the other hand, I suspect that on many occasions, there is a *spirit* operating behind the scenes, driving these dramatic moves to "expose" or undermine generally well-intentioned leaders of key nations, churches, movements, and corporations.

Recently as I taught about the life of David, a seasoned pastor asked about David's peculiar advice to Solomon. He recommended that his young son make arrangements to *dispose of Joab*—even though this was Solomon's cousin and David's former captain of the army (see 1 Kings 2)!

This advice might seem strange and *out of character* for David until you study the life and work of Joab. It really becomes clear when you realize that Solomon would take over the throne at the tender age of nineteen years.

Why was it so important for Solomon to deal with Joab? As we will see in this chapter, the *Joab Spirit* is the *"spirit of disloyalty and betrayal."* Its overriding goal is to *undermine* and *control* a ministry *from within* for the sake of self-ambition and personal preeminence.

If you are a leader, then you already understand why an understanding of the *Joab Spirit* is so crucial to your survival and success. If you aren't, then you should know that this spirit is just as deadly and detrimental to the *followers* and *workers* in a church, organization, or nation as it is to the leaders!

By the time you finish this chapter, you should have a clear understanding of the opposing characteristics of loyalty and the "Joab Spirit." You will understand the *nature* of this spirit, and how it differs from "The Absalom Spirit" in operation. You will recognize the major *characteristics* of "The Joab Spirit" and how you can *deal* with that spirit effectively.

Why is loyalty so important to a church, ministry, or nation? Loyalty is the *mortar*, the binding substance that holds a *church* or *ministry* together. Perhaps part of the problem is our definition of loyalty. It is often confused with faithfulness. Joab was actually "faithful" to David most of the time.

The problem is that loyalty is different from *faithfulness*.

Faithfulness is *action*; it is "something we do." Loyalty is *attitude*; it is "something we are." For example, a man's wife might be "faithful" to her husband in the sense that she doesn't commit adultery with another man or flirt with other men. But she might be *disloyal* to him at the very same time by undermining him among other people with her words or attitudes in public, with the children or inlaws.

Loyalty alone does not qualify a person for ministry. But its *absence*, or the presence of disloyalty, instantly and automatically disqualifies a person from ministry.

Genuine loyalty is constant and true. It does not undermine, but instead supports another by *words, acts and attitudes*. Loyalty is tested in times of trouble and stands firm under fire.

The Joab Spirit Is the Opposite of Loyalty

More than anything else, the Joab Spirit is an *undermining spirit*. It operates from within and behind the scenes. It is extremely subtle and covert, all the while *appearing* to be loyal. It hopes to be and usually is *undetected* for what it really is.

Christian leaders and students of the Bible often talk about *"the Jezebel Spirit"* and *"the Absalom Spirit."* Many books, magazine articles, and church conferences on leadership and government have focused on these adversarial spiritual forces. But we need to be equally aware of *"the Joab Spirit."*

This ancient spirit clearly operated in and influenced the actions of its biblical human namesake, Joab; but it is actually an evil spirit that has influenced human behavior and reinforced evil human attitudes and thought processes since creation. (It is possible that this *"Joab Spirit"* was at work in Cain, influencing and driving him to commit the first murder in human history over jealousy and blind ambition to be first with God. Jude names this spirit after Cain himself.

Compared to the spirits that operated through Jezebel and Absalom, the *Joab Spirit* is:

- more sophisticated
- more dangerous
- more subtle
- more treacherous
- more enduring

To understand what the *Joab Spirit* is, we must first understand the man called Joab. He was David's nephew, the captain of the army, his right hand man, and part of the king's inner circle of counselors, confidants, and leaders.

Joab first came to David at the cave *Adullam* with his two brothers, Abishai and Asahel. All three brothers were part of "David's Mighty Men." His name means *"Yah is Father"* (although it appears he failed to live that way). Joab's name first appears in the Bible in 1 Samuel 26:6, and it is in 1 Chronicles 2:16–17 we learn that Joab's mother is Zeruiah (David's sister).

It is the nature of the Joab Spirit to *infiltrate*. It will work through a person to infiltrate a local church or ministry *"to help out."* Eventually this spirit will birth and nurture betrayal, division, and disloyalty *within the ranks*—often without anyone realizing who was behind it.

The Joab Spirit does all the *right* things for all the *wrong reasons!*

Despite appearing to be King David's "right hand man," Joab (and his brothers) brought David some of the greatest *pain* of his life! Taken collectively, they hurt him more often than anyone else.

Three behaviors and motivations seem to characterize the Joab Spirit.

1. It is preeminently *selfish* and *ambitious*. In practical terms, this spirit always wants to be number one in power, but without a lot of exposure.

2. It is manipulative to an incredible degree. It works constantly *behind the scenes* to have its way, but at the same time *does not actively seek the spotlight*.

3. It has an insatiable *desire for power*, but prefers to exercise it from an *unofficial*

position where it can become known as the true *power behind the throne.*

A person under the influence and control of the Joab Spirit will do his or her work quietly *as long as* he or she is honored and praised, and the leader does not cross him. (This may help to explain, in part, why Joab served David nearly five decades before he was confronted.)

The Joab Spirit works actively in three primary ways to win approval, acquire influence, and cement position in an organization:

- *Currying favor* with key people in the organization
- *Cutting off* any "rising stars" representing a challenge for preeminence
- *Claiming credit* at every opportunity to enhance personal appearance

One of the best ways to understand a thing is to compare and contrast it with similar or competitive persons, places, things, or activities. This process will greatly sharpen one's awareness of the dangerous qualities at work in the Joab Spirit.

Five Key Differences: The Joab Spirit and the Absalom Spirit

Although we've already touched on some characteristics of both of the Joab Spirit and the Absalom Spirit, your understanding of their operations and effects will grow exponentially as you examine *five key differences* between them.

1. Position of Operation

The Absalom Spirit:

- Operates from the "gate," the place of *authority.*

- It *takes* advantage of its authority or position without hesitation or conscience. A person under its influence thinks nothing of "throwing his or her "official weight" around.

- It will boldly lead an *open rebellion.*

- It lets you *know* the one under its influence is your *enemy.*

The Joab Spirit:

- Operates *within the ranks*, in the place of *activity* rather than authority.

- It acts *quietly* and *in secret*, "gnawing away at the inward parts" of the organization, often far from "the palace" or the "leader's office."

- It stays *covert*—or hidden and "under wraps." It would never lead an open rebellion.

- It makes you *think* the one under its influence is your *friend.*

2. Unique Three-fold Purpose

The Absalom Spirit seeks to:

- *Take over* kingly authority.
- *Depose* the reigning king.
- *Rule* in his place.

The Joab Spirit seeks to:

- *Undermine* kingly authority.
- *Emasculate* the reigning king.
- *Rule* behind the throne.

3. Place of Birth

The Absalom Spirit:

- Is often birthed by *an unresolved conflict* which erupts into bitterness and hatred.
- Can be cured.
- Is usually caused by an event.

The Joab Spirit:

- Is usually birthed through *sheer soulish ambition.*
- Sucks the life out of the ministry from within.
- Cannot be cured. (It must be "cast out" and abandoned by its host, just as cancer

must be cut out and every trace of the invading organism "rejected or destroyed" in its victim. Spiritual *death* and *rebirth* are mandatory.)

• It is caused by a character trait.

4. Aggression toward the Leader

The Absalom Spirit:

• Seeks to *break down* the leader's authority through *rebellion.*

• Openly recruits and uses outside assistance.

The Joab Spirit:

• Seeks to *weaken* the leader's authority through subtle undermining.

• Although it is rarely known, this spirit always works to get its own agenda.

5. Ultimate Aim and Methodology

The Absalom Spirit:

• Says, "It is my *right* to be king . . ."

• And, "I will *take* it!"

The Joab Spirit:

• Says "I'm not king, but I will be *in charge* . . ."

- And, "I'll have my way *whatever it takes* and *whoever it hurts!*"

After all of this, you may be thinking, *What else? What more could we possibly learn about Joab?* There is *much* more to cover with this dangerous breed of leader and the spirit that inspires and drives them.

It is time to remove the comparative "Absalom" lens *and* look directly at the appealing and deadly characteristics of the *Joab Spirit*.

Profile of a Joab Leader

Profiling—the practice of developing "characteristic files" for potential criminals, customers, or potential mates—has been a hot topic on talk shows, on Capital Hill, and in civil liberties forums in recent years. In reality, profiling has been a way of life for the human race since Adam first noticed he was different from Eve.

Now it is time to *profile* a Joab, or the leader possibly operating under the influence of *a Joab Spirit*. These characteristics are not offered as fuel for paranoid suspicion, but as information to equip you as a leader. There are **Five General Characteristics of "Joabs":**

1. *Joabs* tend to be *talented and gifted* with genuine *leadership abilities.* However, they often lack personal charisma, divine calling, or

179

godly character necessary for godly leadership.

2. *Joabs* are always ready to step forward to assume *responsibility*.

3. *Joabs* work to endear themselves to *leadership* in times of need or *crisis*.

4. *Joabs* also work to endear themselves to *"the people"* once they land *"on the inside"* with leadership.

5. *Joabs* do everything for one purpose: to further their own agenda, and meet their own need for *preeminence*.

CHAPTER 11

THE SIX *DEADLY* CHARACTERISTICS OF A JOAB LEADER

And I am this day weak, though anointed king; and these men the sons of Zeruiah be *too hard* for me . . . (2 Samuel 3:39a).

As if the five general characteristics aren't enough, there are six *more* characteristics that you need to know about *Joabs*, and they are all deadly. We see all six of these characteristics portrayed clearly in the life of the "original" Joab—David's Joab.

1. Overly Ambitious Spirit

Consuming ambition overtakes human leaders under the influence of the *Joab Spirit*. It is almost impulsive in nature. A Joab leader wrestles constantly with an overly ambitious spirit that threatens to expose him or her to top leaders if it is not held in check.

181

King David made a painful and far-reaching mistake early in his rule when he opened his mouth and committed himself publicly to choose the leader of his army—not by his wisdom, godly counsel, or strategic planning and battle skills— but by his ability to blindly charge into an impossible situation for personal glory.

His nephew, Joab, immediately stepped up to the plate and delivered a home run—leaving Israel's new king with no choice. David had just placed an unprincipled and ambitious killer at the head of his army—and his loyalty was not guaranteed. He was loyal only to himself.

> Then the Jebusites said to David, You shall not come in here! But David took the stronghold of Zion, that is, the City of David.
>
> And David said, *Whoever smites the Jebusites first shall be chief and commander.* **Joab son of Zeruiah** [*David's half sister*] *went up first, and so he was made chief.*
>
> David dwelt in the stronghold; so it was called the City of David.
>
> He built the city from the Millo [a fortification] on around; and Joab repaired and revived the rest of the [old Jebusite] city (1 Chronicles 11:5-8, AMP, emphasis mine).

This driving spirit of ambition in Joab was manifested or revealed in his *soul*, in his thoughts, emotions, and internal wants and desires. It works the same way in everyone influenced or controlled by the *Joab Spirit*.

- A person under the influence of the *Joab Spirit* will quickly grab ministry assignments as opportunities to *get into position to execute his or her own agenda.*

- If you are a leader, **be careful how you delegate responsibilities.** As David discovered, **"Joabs" will always USE ASSIGNMENTS as springboards to something else!** (And it always has to do with "greater prominence.")

2. A Controlling Spirit

Joab's track record with King David is a "biblical text book" on the ways of a *controlling spirit* operating through people. It is almost as if we are watching a classic "gangster movie" as we watch Joab carefully cultivate a "dirt file" on David. He uses embarrassing information as weapons of silent blackmail without hesitation.

As the tale unfolds through 2 Samuel 11, we see Joab entwine himself in David's predicament with Bathsheba. And each time he "helps" David, the "unspoken obligations" and fear factor seem to grow.

David himself provided Joab with his greatest tool for *control* of a king when he sent Joab an incriminating letter seeking his help in murdering an innocent man after seducing the man's wife. David foolishly trusted Joab in his hour of desperation, giving him a handwritten letter saying in essence in his own words, *"Kill Uriah in battle . . . ."*

The controlling spirit ruling Joab's life would never waste such a valuable document. His loyalty isn't for the king, it is for *self*. (NOTE: The Bible does not advocate condoning a leader's sin—it calls for faithful confrontation leading to godly sorrow and repentance, and finally *restoration*.)

Joab, however, wasn't interested in justice or in restoration. He wanted power and *control*. Therefore, he *kept* the letter so he would have *"David in his pocket"* from that day forward!

Don't be deceived. *"Joabs"* in every generation love to *"get something"* on leadership. They will use that embarrassing knowledge to win *"immunity"* from punishment! You will soon notice by their actions that they feel, *"The rules don't apply to me."*

As we see in Joab's life, *control* through blackmail only encourages *a Joab* to think, "I don't have to obey leadership unless it suits *my own purposes!"* (We see proof of that attitude: Joab killed threatening leaders with impunity, including Abner and Amasa. Worst of all, he even defied David's direct command and murdered the king's son in cold blood—in front of witnesses! Beware the *Joab Spirit!*)

3. A Manipulative Spirit

Nearly everyone has dabbled with manipulation sometime in life. Most of us tried to get our way as children, working to manipulate parents, teachers and other children—until we were caught and reprimanded. Some families have made manipulation an art form and a foundation of family relationships (usually with frightening consequences).

However, very *few* people in human history set out to purposely manipulate and deceive *heads of state!* It tends to lead to summary execution or life imprisonment. None of this matters to the *Joab Spirit.* The desire for control is all-consuming, and manipulation is its bond slave.

Joab plotted to manipulate David time and again in his lifetime. Perhaps the greatest act of manipulation took place as Joab played "double agent" to manipulate King David into calling his son, Absalom, out of exile and back to Jerusalem.

> Joab son of Zeruiah knew that the king's heart longed for Absalom. So Joab sent someone to Tekoa and had a wise woman brought from there. He said to her, *"Pretend you are in mourning.* Dress in mourning clothes, and don't use any cosmetic lotions. *Act like* a woman who has spent many days grieving for the dead" (2 Samuel 14:1–2, NIV, emphasis mine).

Joab took action based on his perception that "the king's heart longed for Absalom." Some people may be fooled into believing Joab was acting out of friendship or compassion for his king, but nothing could be further from the truth.

For perhaps the first time in his relationship with his firstborn son, David was saying "No" and enforcing a fixed boundary in his lawless son's life. But he was barely able to overcome his emotions while doing something right. (Yes, Absalom *should* have been given the death penalty under the law for ordering the execution of his own brother, but the exile was at least a small step in the right direction.) Joab saw a fresh soft spot in David's armor and he again acted immediately to weaken David's authority and position himself *above* his king as the power broker in charge!

When a leader has a Joab in the White House, the church office, or the family business, that leader should be prepared to fight every battle on *two fronts!*

Most of the attention always seems to go to the challenge, opponent, or threat coming from the front side in full view. Unfortunately for leaders employing or entrusting a Joab, the most deadly fight is forming right behind them under the skilled guidance of their most trusted associate, organizational officer, or family member. And disguise, illusion, pretense, and apparent good will are *always* involved. Nothing is as it seems, but the motives are all too predictable. His motive was blatant ambition for power and control, but he had no problem painting it any color necessary, dressing it up in mourning clothes, or waving a patriot's flag.

The end (or the goal) *always* justifies *any means* (or method) *necessary* for a Joab.

Joab the master manipulator thought nothing of plotting to deceive a cousin, a king or God's anointed—they were all one and the same to him. David's wishes amounted only to an obstacle to be overcome by any means, or a "meal ticket" to greater power.

In this case, Joab set out to create a grand illusion, a sophisticated scam of royal proportions that would directly affect the nation of Israel for generations to come. Many translations of these key Bible passages simply tell us that Joab "sent to Tekoah and fetched a wise woman" and stop there. Since we are dealing with a Joab, you should know there is more to this than meets the uncritical eye.

As we noted earlier in Chapter 7, this was no "wise" woman. She was a professional actress who was artful and cunning in her ways. She had such a reputation for her skill in running a "con or confidence game" that wily Joab knew exactly whom to call and how to reach her. She was an expert at building "confidence" in her sham identities and manufactured stories. Although she approached David with a make-believe story just as Nathan had done years earlier, she was *not* sent by God, she was *not* a prophet or prophetess, nor did she have the best interests of David or her nation at heart!

Tekoah was also the home of Ira, one of King David's thirty mighty men (2 Samuel 23:26), who may have been the unwitting source guiding Joab's men to this con woman in his wilderness village about twelve miles away from Jerusalem. At a future time, the remote village would redeem itself through another native son, Amos the shepherd-prophet (Amos 1:1).

It took a while, but as you read through the fourteenth chapter of 2 Samuel, you come upon the nineteenth verse where "the light bulb finally came on" for David, and he pinned down the actress and pinpointed the *source* of the charade designed to deceive and coerce him.

Joab was pressuring David to do something unethical and unwise that would finally *sever* the hearts of the people from their king.

> The king asked, *"Isn't the hand of Joab with you in all this?"*
>
> The woman answered, "As surely as you live, my lord the king, no one can turn to the right or to the left from anything my lord the king says. *Yes, it was your servant Joab who instructed me to do this and who put all these words into the mouth of your servant. Your servant Joab did this to change the present situation.* My lord has wisdom like that of an angel of God—he knows everything that happens in the land."
>
> The king said to Joab, "Very well, I will do it. Go, bring back the young man Absalom."
>
> Joab fell with his face to the ground to pay

him honor, and he blessed the king. Joab said, "Today your servant knows that he has found favor in your eyes, my lord the king, because the king has granted his servant's request" (2 Samuel 14:19–22, NIV, emphasis mine).

There is something incredibly sad about this scene where David capitulates and says in what must have been great weariness of spirit, "Very well, I will do it. Go, bring back the young man Absalom." David had just confirmed his suspicion that the whole affair was a sordid charade meant to deceive him. The paid liar openly confessed that Joab was behind the whole thing! David's response was basically to sigh and surrender.

Joab only pretended to be a "peace-maker" between David and Absalom. His real motive was to benefit himself using one of several strategies:

1. He would show himself to be *"wiser"* than King David.

2. He would move the up-and-coming young would-be king, Absalom, *into position for power* and would benefit himself in these ways:

   • by currying his favor since he would probably ascend to the throne soon by force or later by family bloodline;

   • by using him as a distraction to keep David *"off balance"* so that Joab could

189

move to consolidate even more power and influence behind the throne.

He did all this to make *himself* look good at the legitimate king's expense. He was "playing both ends against the middle" while maneuvering to benefit himself no matter who came out on top. In the end, Joab intended for *Joab* to be on top. By winning this battle of the wills with King David and by bringing back the ever-popular Prince Absalom, Joab only strengthened *himself* in the royal palace for possible future opportunities.

And finally, in the familiar pattern later followed by organized crime bosses in countless future cultures and eras, by gathering "blackmail" material and holding it over the leader's head, Joab established very real leverage and preeminence in the nation's political and military power circles.

4. A Jealous Spirit

The *Joab Spirit* seems to have a built-in "radar" for competition and potential rivals. It will permit no one—no matter how unlikely or how prominent the candidate—to be promoted or honored above its own place or position.

After Joab had murdered David's son, Absalom, in open defiance to his direct command, he then berated David for mourning over his son and offending the men of Israel who had fought for David.

The king listened enough to take his seat of

authority and win the hearts of the men to himself, but he had finally had his fill of Joab. He sent a message through two loyal priests to Joab's cousin, Amasa, telling him he would take Joab's place: "Are you not my own flesh and blood? May God deal with me, be it ever so severely, if from now on you are not the commander of my army in place of Joab" (2 Samuel 19:13, NIV).

Then David sent Amasa out on his first assignment, to round up David's army. Unfortunately for Amasa, he took longer to do the job than David had given him (see 2 Samuel 20:5). In the next sentence, David turns to somebody who was there, Abishai, Joab's brother.

By the time Amasa finally showed up, Joab and his brother Abishai had already raised the army and were at the head. That opened the door for Joab to take care of the "competition" and secure his place in David's government—whether he liked it or not. It had all of the trappings of a modern-day Mafia execution:

> So Joab's men and the Kerethites and Pelethites and all the mighty warriors went out under the command of Abishai. They marched out from Jerusalem to pursue Sheba son of Bicri.
>
> While they were at the great rock in Gibeon, *Amasa came to meet them.* [A leader should never be late.] Joab was wearing his military tunic, and strapped over it at his waist was a belt with a dagger in its

sheath. As he stepped forward, it dropped out of its sheath [on purpose].

Joab said to Amasa, "How are you, my brother?" Then *Joab took Amasa by the beard with his right hand to kiss him. Amasa was not on his guard against the dagger in Joab's hand, and Joab plunged it into his belly, and his intestines spilled out on the ground.* Without being stabbed again, Amasa died. Then Joab and his brother Abishai pursued Sheba son of Bicri (2 Samuel 20:7–10, NIV, emphasis mine).

If there are any doubts that this was a public execution purposely done in front of the troops, then consider what happened next: *"One of Joab's men stood beside Amasa and said, 'Whoever favors Joab, and whoever is for David, let him follow Joab!'"* (2 Samuel 20:11, NIV). Joab brutally murdered Amasa as a bloody warning to everyone watching the scene—"There is *only one* leader around here, and that leader is me!"

The *Joab Spirit* operating in a man or a woman will *derail, defame, and destroy* anyone and anything that threatens its position of power in an organization. That is why you cannot trust a Joab with *new converts* who have talent and ability! He will find a way to *"neutralize them"* to maintain the status quo.

5. A Grief to Leadership

The fifth deadly characteristic of a Joab leader is the willingness and tendency to bring *grief* to the leader in charge, and anyone else associated with leadership. One of the *many* incidents in David's long association with Joab clearly reveals how Joab grieved King David through his lawless actions of self-preservation, self-promotion and personal revenge. Consider David's sad statement concerning Joab and his brothers:

> And I am this day weak, though anointed king; and these men the sons of Zeruiah [Joab and Abishai] be *too hard* for me: the LORD shall reward the doer of evil according to his wickedness (2 Samuel 3:39, emphasis mine).

David's declaration over his violent cousins came at the end of a long internal war between his men and the followers of Saul's last living son (Ishbosheth). Abner was a seasoned warrior who served as general for Ishbosheth's army. When he realized he was fighting against God as well as fighting a losing battle, he approached David (who was king only over Judah at the time) to make a peace covenant. David sent him away in peace after Abner agreed to help win over the elders of Israel and unify the nation.

When Joab heard that King David had met privately with Abner, he was enraged because Abner had just killed his younger brother,

Abishai, during their last battle. He sent messengers after Abner in the king's name (without telling David), and then called him aside as if to talk to him. Then he stabbed him to death with one blow.

What general kills someone with whom his supreme leader has just negotiated a war-ending, nation-healing covenant? A Joab leader—that is the kind of leader who thinks nothing of bringing untold grief and pain to his leader as long as it suits his own personal need for advancement or revenge.

We should notice three things that stand out in David's relationship with Joab in this incident:

First, David did well in that he *publicly* mourned for Abner, demonstrating his personal love for the murdered leader. This was more than a mere political ploy; David really did love and respect Abner as one of the greatest military leaders and heroes in Israel in his lifetime. However, it *also* had real political consequences because Abner was also a hero to the majority of Israelites who were under the rule of Saul's son at the time. Joab's reckless act of murder in a family vendetta could have ignited another long round of bloody battles.

Second, David also made sure Abner was honored and buried as a national hero. In doing so, he helped unite both the people of Judah and those from the other tribes under Israel. He was also making a point to Joab (it didn't work—and it rarely *does* with a true Joab).

Third, David *failed* to genuinely punish Joab

for his lawlessness, disloyalty, and above all, for the premeditated *murder* of Abner. The king demoted Joab from his chief position over his army, but everyone (including David) knew he could and would reclaim the position any time he decided to do so.

David also made Joab mourn for Abner, which basically means he made him attend the public funeral. Yet, none of these things really mattered to Joab or even slowed him down. He knew David wouldn't kill him or even fire him.

There are two things about the *"Joab Spirit"* that bring leaders grief:

1. The *Joab Spirit* makes people who yield to it think they are *"special"* and *"above the rules."* This is a *"must have"* position for Joabs.

2. People operating under the influence of the *Joab Spirit* think the biblically blessed qualities of tenderheartedness, mercy and forgiveness are *undesirable* traits for any leader to have! They respect only those leaders who appear to be *tough, professional,* and *ruthless.* (That would appear to leave out Jesus Christ, the apostle Paul, and most if not all of the Twelve Apostles. All of them were tough, but few if any were even interested in being "professional." The work of Jesus on the Cross and His gospel of love totally rules out ruthless!)

6. A Disrespectful Spirit

When the *Joab Spirit* dominates a human soul, it makes the person disrespectful toward those in authority, while demanding that total respect be shown to him or her. We've already discussed Joab's violent and premeditated murder of Absalom while he was suspended weaponless and totally helpless from a tree. We revisit that incident again to illustrate the royal *disrespect* demonstrated in Joab's murderous act.

> When one of the men saw this, he told Joab, "I just saw Absalom hanging in an oak tree."
>
> Joab said to the man who had told him this, "What! You saw him? Why didn't you strike him to the ground right there? Then I would have had to give you ten shekels of silver and a warrior's belt."
>
> But the man replied, "Even if a thousand shekels were weighed out into my hands, I would not lift my hand against the king's son. *In our hearing the king commanded you and Abishai and Ittai, 'Protect the young man Absalom for my sake.'* [KJV – BEWARE that none touch the young man Absalom.] And if I had put my life in jeopardy—and nothing is hidden from the king—you would have kept your distance from me."
>
> Joab said, "I'm not going to wait like this for you." So he took three javelins in his

hand and plunged them into Absalom's heart while Absalom was still alive in the oak tree. And ten of Joab's armorbearers surrounded Absalom, struck him and killed him (2 Samuel 18:10–15, NIV, emphasis mine).

There is no limit to the "Joab Spirit." It will do anything to further its own agenda!

Notice two things this passage reveals about Joab's nature:

1. The brave but unnamed soldier *knew* that if he had harmed Absalom, then Joab would have abandoned him to suffer the consequences, or he might even have killed him to pretend he was defending David's son.

2. Joab rushed off to kill Absalom *himself* before Absalom could get free from the oak tree.

How to Deal with the "Joab Spirit"

It is *never easy* to deal with the *Joab Spirit*, but it is *possible!* However, you can only deal effectively with the *Joab Spirit* when *seven things* are in place:

197

A. Make sure your resolve is compelling!

You must know that you have heard from God! Due to the power and influence wielded by the *Joab Spirit*, even those closest and dearest to you may be "under the influence" of this person's persuasive brew. Your chief counselors may be measuring your desk for your successor with the "Joab degree" in Success at Any Cost. Your own spouse and children may be wearing Joab stickers and promoting his or her views over yours! (Never underestimate the power of this spirit to sway the minds of people who aren't seeking God's counsel and walking in His power as they should).

You must be fully convinced that "it must be done!" And you must be equally sure it must be done *now*, not later. *Later* translates into *never* when Joab is in the picture.

Understand that people will misunderstand. By definition, it takes a leader to take people to a place where they normally won't go. That goes "double or more" when it comes to confronting a Joab Spirit! People will not understand. Accept it and plan for it. And understand that it also means you will *"look bad"* to some if not all of the people around you or looking to you for leadership.

Know that once you start, there is *no turning back!* Don't weaken; hold your ground. It will only get worse if you do.

Jesus Christ knew He was challenging the authority of the "Father of all Joabs" by taking down Satan, the prince of the power of the air.

Perhaps that is why He warned a young volunteer for the War of the Cross, "No one who puts his hand to the plow *and looks back* is fit for service in the kingdom of God" (Luke 9:62, NIV, emphasis mine).

B. Be sure your life is clean (and blackmail proof)!

Your life must be free from moral compromise. The *Joab Spirit* is a master of blackmail, underhanded schemes, and sinister plotting. He thrives the most where the senior leader's moral and ethical life is most cloudy and questionable. That gives him or her "lots to work with."

There must be no "Uriah's" in your history with Joab. If you have used the considerable "strong-arm and forceful manipulation skills " of the Joab Spirit for your own gain or advantage, remember that this spirit never forgets and never fails to call upon a "sin-debt" to be paid, usually with even more sin. When you deal with a Joab Spirit, you are dealing with "the original Mafia family" from hell.

If you *do* have a *Uriah favor* in your history, you can count on a person operating under a *Joab Spirit* to choose the worst possible moment to play that *"sleeve card"* against you—pulling out that "dirty little secret" at the moment most damaging to you and most beneficial for him or her!

(If you *do* have a secret in your moral closet, the best thing to do is to *repent* immediately, *reveal it* openly yourself, *make amends* as you are able, and *cast yourself upon the mercy and provision of God*—just as David did.)

The best path is to *make sure the Joab Spirit has nothing on you*—morally, ethically, or in any other way!

C. Make sure your authority is clear.

Your authority to deal with *any* major problem in the ministry, organization, or group must be *understood by all involved*. And *you* must understand that "only David can deal with Joab!"

Only the senior leader can deal with a high-ranking leader who is in the wrong. This is especially true for one operating with a *Joab Spirit!* This is one leadership problem that cannot ever be *delegated*. (The *Joab Spirit* is especially lethal to leaders of equal or lower rank who seek to bring correction or resist its influence on their own authority.)

All involved must clearly understand that your *authority* is of legal and proper origin. Authority that is *usurped* or seized illegally from another or by your own decision apart from senior leadership is rooted in rebellion and lawlessness.

Once this is understood, it should be clear to all that the actions you take are *not* being taken for personal *revenge*. On the contrary, your decisions and actions are being taken *"for the good of all"* (which is the proper basis for genuine leaders exercising legal authority under God).

200

D. Your motive must be *chaste.*

By "chaste" in this situation, I refer to the quality of purity in thought and deed.

Make sure your plans, decisions, and actions are ethical, or are done for the right reason. Make sure that *you understand the true issues* and are not caught up in the chaos and confusion that often cloud the thinking of many in times of crisis, conflict, or confrontation.

Take time in prayer and meditation to *confirm that your attitude is uncontaminated* by perceived insults, conflicts, or personal conflicts of interest of any kind. Above all, make sure you are *not acting out of anger.*

Always take precautions to operate and act legally—be legally correct with both God and man. If questioned at any point in the process of dealing with the *Joab Spirit,* you should be able to answer honestly, "This is for wrongs done to *us,* not for wrongs done to *me.*"

(Remember, the original Joab was quick to kill over personal wrongs or offenses while using his official position and influence to help make it happen—he calmly killed General Abner as well as Amasa, the man David appointed to replace Joab!)

E. Ensure that your timing is correct.

Don't underestimate anyone under the influence of the *Joab Spirit.* David waited forty-seven years to rein in Joab *because of the Uriah incident.* Yet there was more at stake than merely reluctance to "be found out." In reality, David's sin with Uriah actually did "come out" and become common knowledge in Israel, and it cost him dearly. His delay in dealing with Joab was probably rooted in at least three reasons:

Joab *was* a useful if deadly ally for the king of Israel—as long as his lethal tendencies were directed away from David and his fellow Israelites.

Second, David was, himself, a mighty warrior. He *may* have felt he could deal with Joab himself if necessity demanded it.

Third, and my chief point here, is that Joab was too dangerous to tackle blindly and without careful preparation.

David timed it well. While *he* managed to function with Joab *most* of the time, *it was clear to him and to the people that young Solomon—a man of wisdom but not of war—was no match for Joab.* This dangerous man would have to be removed from power before he could influence the fate of the nation or kill Solomon once King David stepped aside or died.

F. Be certain that your methods are *kind.*

Your methods of leadership and correction must be sympathetic and not destructive. David's methods reflected his conviction that his responsibility was *to serve Israel, not merely to kill or remove Joab.*

One of the practical ways to demonstrate kindness in a high-profile demotion or corrective removal of a leader is to conduct the confrontation and administer the consequence quietly without being loud, nervous, or vindictive.

Perhaps you have heard of churches or ministries "demonizing" employees who were laid off or released from their positions. Some unfortunate individuals have been pointedly "escorted" to their desks by security staff, supervised as they cleaned out their desks, and then paraded in public shame all the way to their cars and monitored until they were out of sight of the property.

This is "leadership by paranoia," and totally opposite from the biblical leadership we see in the lives of Jesus, Paul, Peter, and James.

Rather than publicly humiliate a subordinate leader who has been too harsh or too manipulative to remain in your church staff or ministry, it would be better for your leader and leadership team to talk to him privately and then officially release him from his position at 4:45 p.m. Friday afternoon in the parking lot (before the other employees and staff get off) with a generous severance check and the best letter of recommendation possible.

In everything, keep your focus on healing, not on hurting. Even Joab was a descendant of Abraham, Isaac, and Jacob. Even your worst nightmare of an employee or staff member was included in Jesus Christ's miracle on the cross!

G. Godly conduct produces desirable consequences.

You can rarely measure the value of the actions and decisions you make until later, when everything has been said and done. A good leader loves everyone, even those he or she must correct or even fire from their positions.

The real test comes afterwards. One way we can assess our conduct is by the way people react to the final outcome. It is hard to imagine a herd of sheep experiencing peace at the height of a battle between the shepherd and a marauding wolf, coyote, or lion. You must check the sheep later, after the noise of the battle has died down and the source of danger has been removed.

I think I would want to hear people commenting with conviction, *"He did what he had to do, but he did not enjoy it."* It helps when you hear people say, *"She is a strong but fair leader."*

One of the greatest principles revealed in the comments of higher level staff members "in the know" after a staff adjustment may show up in a statement such as, *"That hurt him more than it hurt us—or even Joab."* If a good leader loves everyone, including those he must correct or remove from a key position, then that leader *hurts and sympathizes with* the pain felt by others. Yet he still does the right thing!

Finally, when a senior leader such as a pastor, college president, judge, or the President of the United States takes the right action to remove someone with the *Joab Spirit,* more than anything else he or she will probably hear this said quite often: *"He could (should) have done that a long time ago, but he did what he had to do, not what he wanted to do."*

Few opponents you will face as a leader in life and ministry will ever match the potential evil and cunning demonstrated by the *Joab Spirit.* Perhaps it is dangerous precisely because it so closely matches the devious ways and consuming ambition seen in the senior cherub's astounding aspiration to assume God's throne—and his ability to persuade a full third of the angels in heaven to join his outlandish plot!

Remember that people under the influence of the *Joab Spirit* are skilled and driven to undermine authority because they are led by a *spirit of disloyalty.* It is also a spirit of ambition and *preeminence,* and it is far more *dangerous* than the *Absalom Spirit!*

In summary, the deadly characteristics identifying the *Joab Spirit* are:

- Overly ambitious
- Controlling
- Manipulative
- Jealous of place
- Grief to leadership
- Disrespectful

If you must deal with the *Joab Spirit*, you should do so only if your:

- Resolve is compelling
- Life is clean
- Authority is clear
- Motive is chaste
- Timing is correct
- Methods are kind

If you do things God's way and with God's heart and motives, then when it is over people will say of you what they said of David: "He did what he *had* to do, not what he *wanted* to do."

CHAPTER 12

DAVIDíS LEGACY

God's Final Word

*Now the days of David drew nigh that he
should die; and he charged Solomon his son,
saying*

*I go the way of all the earth: be thou strong
therefore, and shew thyself a man*

1 Kings 2:1–2

David's days were drawing to a close. As a
young man fresh from his father's sheep fields, he
had singlehandedly defeated the Philistine cham-
pion, Goliath. He had outlasted every enemy who
rose against him, including King Saul and his
armies.

The great Psalmist of Israel was about to "go the
way of all men." His eyes were dim; his body was
perpetually cold as the fires of his earthly life grew
weak. It was almost time for him to *"go home."*

For the man or woman of God, death is not
defeat! It is merely a *door* from the constricted realm

of time to the boundless realm of eternity where the Creator dwells. It is the final passage from mortality to immortality, and for every follower of Jesus Christ, it is also a door from sin, sickness and sorrow to eternal life, light and everlasting love in His presence.

King David knew all this, even though many of his contemporaries had no hope of life beyond the *grave*. In his lifetime, David was a standout, a unique beacon signaling the coming miracle of the cross and the desire of God to walk *intimately* with ordinary men and women.

In an era when the "fear" or awe of God was everything, David demonstrated the higher privilege of *loving and being loved by* God, and of walking with Him for a lifetime.

David himself once wrote:

> As for me, I will behold thy face in righteousness: I shall be satisfied, when I awake, with thy likeness (Psalm 17:15).

Yes, David knew what awaited him and he had peace about his future after death. However, he was still very concerned about his *legacy*, and about his son to whom he was leaving it! Although he was departing this earth, there were many "loose ends" in the form of enemies who still posed potentially deadly dangers for his son, Solomon, and for the peace of Israel.

His final thoughts were of the future work of God, particularly of the "house" he wanted to build for God. So no one should have been surprised to learn that David's final advice to Solomon was both *spiritual* and *practical*.

> And keep the charge of the LORD thy God, to walk in his ways, to keep his statutes, and his commandments, and his judgments, and his testimonies, as it is written in the law of Moses, that thou mayest prosper in all that thou doest, and whithersoever thou turnest thyself:
>
> That the LORD may continue his word which he spake concerning me, saying, If thy children take heed to their way, to walk before me in truth with all their heart and with all their soul, there shall not fail thee (said he) a man on the throne of Israel (1 Kings 2:3–4).

David's Spiritual Advice to Solomon

When Solomon arrived at his father's bedside, King David immediately launched into a careful outline of his *core values* to his son. He was speaking from painful experience when he told Solomon never to stray from this *center*.

This kingly counsel stems from God's prophetic declaration to David concerning His covenant commitment to him and to his descendants. (We dealt with this in Chapter One, "What To Do When God Says 'No'!") But as with all divine covenants, this was *conditional* upon godly living in alignment with four cardinal truths. These first-in-importance truths apply to all of us in good times and bad. Here they are in condensed form:

1. Keep the *charge* of the Lord to live uprightly. Your life should be marked by *decency.*

2. Walk humbly in the paths of righteousness. In other words, be a "law-abiding citizen" who *lives in community with fairness and equity.*

3. Obey God's *edicts* and commandments. Be faithful and courageous to your unique calling and *"be the best that you can be."*

4. Love His *law* and be loyal to His desires. Live in and with integrity. *"Be on the inside what you claim to be on the outside."*

These bedrock truths form:

- The street to solid *success*
- The path to personal *power*
- The highway to high *honor*
- The road to real *respect*

This is the only way to assure God's grace and favor because it is *our part* of the Covenant. It requires *humility, obedience,* and *love.* David was careful to remind Solomon that he *must live a life of integrity* before God and His people.

This is great *spiritual* advice from a loving father to his son. How many problems could be avoided altogether today if more fathers gave this kind of godly advice to their sons and daughters? What, exactly, qualifies as "godly advice"?

David's Practical Advice to Solomon

"Now you yourself know what Joab son of Zeruiah did to me—what he did to the two commanders of Israel's armies, Abner son of Ner and Amasa son of Jether. He killed them, shedding their blood in peacetime as if in battle, and with that blood stained the belt around his waist and the sandals on his feet. Deal with him according to your wisdom, but do not let his gray head go down to the grave in peace.

"But show kindness to the sons of Barzillai of Gilead and let them be among those who eat at your table. They stood by me when I fled from your brother Absalom.

"And remember, you have with you Shimei son of Gera, the Benjamite from Bahurim, who called down bitter curses on me the day I went to Mahanaim. When he came down to meet me at the

Jordan, I swore to him by the LORD: 'I
will not put you to death by the sword.'
But now, do not consider him innocent.
You are a man of wisdom; you will know
what to do to him. Bring his gray head
down to the grave in blood" (1 Kings
2:5–9, NIV).

When you read this historic Bible passage for
the first time, your modern, peacetime ideas of
right and wrong may kick in with the unspoken
objection, "This is just angry and hateful revenge!"
However, there is *more* to this final instruction than
meets the eye, and it is far deeper and less sinister
than some commentators have believed.

In fact, the major element of David's life for
which God said of him: "He is a man after my own
heart" was his ability to *forgive* and *forget* wrongs
done to him.

King David gave this advice to Solomon for a
far more important reason than merely to get belat-
ed revenge on his own personal enemies. David
had spent a lifetime growing wise in the ways of
life-and-death struggle on the battle field and in the
royal court of intrigue. Now at the end of his life
and royal reign, King David was determined to
help preserve *Solomon's* life long enough to secure
the Israelite empire for the purposes of *God*.

David's spiritual advice (in the first few verses of 1 Kings chapter two) was designed to influence Solomon's *personal* character to accomplish
God's Kingdom purposes. His practical advice,

however, was designed to influence Solomon's *political* circumstances to accomplish God's Kingdom purposes.

In a way, we see a picture of this in the life and mission of Jesus Christ. He ministered continuously for three and a half years from the Word of God, going about "doing good and healing" in miraculous signs and wonders. But in the end, His "political" role would be much more brutal and would bring a *final end* to the chief enemy of His Father in Heaven. (This solution would *also* involve violence and blood, but in the greater Son of David's case, it would be His own.)

David knew that Solomon was entering a lion's den inhabited and essentially ruled by the most feared killer and schemer in all of Israel. Kindness, patience, and negotiation meant nothing to him—he only recognized and respected strength. Solomon had nothing that Joab would respect or fear once David was gone from the scene. You see a portion of David's thinking revealed in his first advice concerning Joab in 1 Kings 2:5–6.

King David had endured more problems and grief from Joab than from anyone else in his entire life—*including murderous and insecure King Saul!* This powerful man with an even more powerful ambition and appetite for power openly *defied* and *tricked* David time after time to get his own way—in spite of David's clearly communicated wishes and commands. As you look at the list of Joab's "accomplishments," ask yourself whether or not you believe in "capital punishment" for these crimes:

213

- Joab personally murdered *Abner*, David's commanding general, in cold blood right in front of witnesses.

- Joab personally murdered *Amasa*, another commander, also in cold blood and in front of witnesses.

- Joab even murdered *Absalom*, David's own son, in front of witnesses; and then had his own loyal band of soldiers further mutilate the body in full view of David's troops. And Joab did all of this despite King David's direct command. How could he get away with it? The master manipulator had the *"letter of Uriah"* in his pocket!

- In the end, Joab actually joined David's fourth son, *Adonijah*, in his open rebellion and coup attempt to steal the throne from Solomon, whom David had personally chosen to succeed him.

These violent and lawless acts made it clear that once David was out of the way, Joab would inevitably become an overt *enemy and threat* to Solomon. That made Joab a threat to God's plan through David. So the only reason David offered such seemingly violent advice to his son was to thwart that inevitability.

David's second piece of advice concerned *Shimei*, the extreme supporter and relative of Saul who violently cursed David as the king fled for his life during the rebellion of Absalom (see 1 Kings 2:8–9). This man thought nothing of "touching God's anointed." In fact, he did what no decent man does, even to his worst enemy. He essentially *"kicked David while he was down."* The problem wasn't merely his insult; it was his deep heart motive. He wanted David *dead*, not merely removed from power! He was a relative of Saul and wanted David's family out of the way perhaps in the hope that he might have some opportunity for power.

(Even in the modern United States or in Great Britain, security forces such as the Secret Service take a very dim view of threats against the President. People can dislike, protest, and shout political slogans all day, but verbal threats or intent to do bodily harm are crimes against the state.)

Some things are predictable in every era. David wasn't surprised to find that once he returned to power after Absalom's failure, Shimei showed up to beg for his worthless life. *"Forgiving David"* allowed his chief critic to live, *against* the advice of other leaders.

However, although David was forgiving, he wasn't stupid or naïve. He knew what was in Shimei's heart, and he knew this old rebel would rise up against Solomon at the first opportunity. So he counseled his son to keep Shimei under close *surveillance* (house arrest) until the day he died.

(Modern governments also closely monitor people and groups suspected to be hostile or potentially dangerous to leaders or to the public good. This is how so many terrorist "sleeper cells" have been broken up in the years since Islamic extremists attacked the World Trade Center on 9-11 in 2001.)

Third, David gave Solomon some practical advice concerning *Barzillai*, the powerful old Gileadite who helped David against Absalom (see 1 Kings 2:7). Only Barzillai had enough courage to help King David when he was fleeing for his life from Absalom's forces. David desperately needed shelter, supplies and friendship, and it was Barzillai who was his *"friend when in need"* when nobody else wanted or dared to help (see 2 Samuel 19:31–39).

By this time, Barzillai was advanced in age, so David asked Solomon to make Barzillai's sons *"friends of the Royal Court."* This honor of *"dining at the royal table"* was not referring to shared meal-times with King Solomon. It meant that they would enjoy regular support from the royal treasury—they were virtual *"Knights of the King."* (They would share this position with Jonathan's son, *Mephibosheth*.)

The wisdom and advice King David shared with his son was both general and practical, and it would help to safely and securely establish Solomon as king of Israel in David's place. It is clear that without it, young Solomon would have failed in his early years.

Once David delivered his *legacy* to Solomon, he died.

Solomon Followed David's Advice

Solomon took immediate and drastic action based solely upon the instructions from his father, King David. These actions showed his strength and determination to rule in his father's place. They also made him *successful* in his early reign.

As the newly crowned king of Israel, Solomon's first order of business was to deal with the other claimant to the throne: *Adonijah*. King David did not counsel Solomon to harm his half-brother. After all, Adonijah was still David's own son, but Israel's greatest king was thinking about God's covenant and about his legacy.

Adonijah had already been warned, and King David had made it abundantly clear to the entire nation whom he had chosen to take his throne after his death. Adonijah would bear full responsibility for any choices or actions he took after such clear warnings. As for David's counsel to Solomon on the matter, his advice to "be strong and brook no rivals" was very clear.

When Adonijah learned that Solomon had been crowned king, he fled to the tabernacle, gripped "the horns of the altar," and refused to leave unless Solomon would swear not to kill him with the sword. Solomon went to extra lengths to extend mercy while also sending a crystal-clear message to his ambitious older half-brother. He essentially told Adonijah to *"stand down"* and to abandon his grand idea of *usurping* the throne of David from his hands.

217

Solomon replied, "If he shows himself to be a worthy man, not a hair of his head will fall to the ground; but if evil is found in him, he will die." Then King Solomon sent men, and they brought him down from the altar. And Adonijah came and bowed down to King Solomon, and Solomon said, "Go to your home" (1 Kings 1:52–53, NIV).

It seems Adonijah was indeed Absalom's proud younger brother, because the king's warning didn't sink in. He had his own ideas and ambitions, and in spite of David's wishes, Adonijah schemed again from his headquarters in Hebron to steal Solomon's throne.

Like Absalom before him, Adonijah was handsome and striking in appearance. And even worse, David's flawed parenting skills apparently had only reinforced some inherent flaws present in his son's character. The Bible's description of this situation is sadly haunting:

Now Adonijah, whose mother was Haggith, *put himself forward* [KJV—exalted himself] and said, "I will be king." *So he got chariots and horses ready, with fifty men to run ahead of him. His father had never interfered with him by asking, "Why do you behave as you do?"* He was also very handsome and was born next after Absalom (1 Kings 1:5–6, NIV, emphasis mine).

Where was this man during his older brother's ill-fated attempt to seize the throne of David? He was falling for the same blind ambition, and he even took the first page out of Absalom's failed "play book" when he called for a chariot and horses plus *fifty men to run ahead of him!* (See 2 Samuel 15:1.)

David wasn't even dead yet when Adonijah called for the horse-drawn limousine, publicly declared himself king, and planned his coronation celebration party. However, he still had considerable political skills as a schemer. Before Adonijah fully revealed his plan, he had talked secretly with two of the most powerful men in Israel at the time and recruited their help for his coup attempt.

- Joab, the grizzled and manipulative general of David's armies, ruled the military with an iron fist. But he was loyal only to himself, and since David was drawing his last breaths, he decided Adonijah was the rising star he would follow.

- Abiathar the high priest was the second man Adonijah courted for support. He was Israel's highest ranking and most senior religious leader, but it appears that his former loyalty to David dating from their days as fugitives together in the cave Adullam no longer suited his political aspirations.

According to the Bible, there *were* respected leaders and family members who remained loyal to the aged king and to Solomon. First on the list were the old prophet, Nathan, and David's wife and the mother of Solomon, Bath-Sheba. When Nathan learned of Adonijah's scheme, he immediately contacted Bath-Sheba and told her his unique plan to inform King David (see 1 Kings 1:11–14).

Bath-Sheba broke the news, and then Nathan timed his arrival to reinforce her warning. But just before Nathan arrived, Bath-Sheba sealed her warning with an urgent appeal that virtually any national leader would find difficult to ignore:

> "My lord the king, *the eyes of all Israel are on you,* to learn from you who will sit on the throne of my lord the king after him. Otherwise, as soon as my lord the king is laid to rest with his fathers, *I and my son Solomon will be treated as criminals"* (1 Kings 1:20–21, NIV, emphasis mine).

Nathan carefully repeated the core events the king had just heard from Bath-Sheba, and then he specifically noted that Adonijah had *not* invited:

- *Solomon,* the loyal and godly son David had previously chosen to succeed him to the throne of Israel (most of the "king's sons" *were* invited to Adonijah's coronation party)

- *Benaiah,* the extremely loyal general David had just appointed as head of the army in Joab's place

- *Zadok* the High Priest, who *shared* high priestly duties with *Abiathar*

David carefully instructed each one of his leaders what they were to do, and when they followed the king's instructions it was very clear that his will could not and would not be overturned or misunderstood. To use a common judicial expression, it was "an airtight case."

We know King David's plan was effective because *immediately* the support of Joab and Abiathar melted away from Adonijah, the prince-who-would-be-king. All of the king's sons and the high level military commanders who attended the dinner also quietly faded into the shadows while Adonijah made a high-speed run for the protection of "the horns of the altar."

Even after all of this took place and Solomon had extended a pardon and mercy toward his presumptuous rival, ambitious Adonijah still tried to lift himself above Solomon by using a slick *trick* that must have been transparent to everyone! He went to Bath-Sheba and asked her to approach her son and ask that *Abishag*, the beautiful Shunamite woman who took care of frail David in his final days, become his wife.

Solomon immediately understood the motive behind Adonijah's subtle and treacherous move. In the ancient Near Eastern culture of his day, this stunt was just as despicable and disgusting as Absalom's insulting decision to sleep with the women in his own father's royal harem at the urging of Ahithophel! (See 2 Samuel 16:2–22.)

Adonijah was still up to his old tricks, and Solomon was enraged. There was no need to convene a court or conduct a hearing. Adonijah was already living under the ancient equivalent of a "suspended sentence." The death penalty could automatically be invoked any time Adonijah broke the conditions of his conditional pardon—and he had just crossed the line.

Solomon decided it was time to eliminate this threat to his empire and he immediately dispatched Benaiah, the commander of his army, to execute his treasonous older brother. Benaiah did so without hesitation.

Solomon's Second Move to Secure Power

With his first and most dangerous threat removed from the picture, Solomon then dealt with the second serious threat his father had warned him about. Abiathar, the high priest, was clearly guilty of intrigue or conspiracy against Solomon because he had publicly supported Adonijah's foolish attempt to seize the crown from David and Solomon. He actually served as Adonijah's spiritual adviser during the attempted insurrection (evidently, his advice wasn't very good).

This was an especially sad duty because Abiathar (now in his final years), had been loyal to

David throughout the reign of Saul and served the people in the cave Adullam as their priest in exile. Abiathar was there with Zadok when David accepted the crown of Israel. He was there with David when he and his family fled Jerusalem with the ark of the Covenant when Absalom led the rebellion against his father. Had old Abiathar not joined Adonijah's futile attempt to seize David's crown and usurp Solomon, then he would have been kept on as honored priest until his death.

Yet, because Abiathar *did* conspire against King Solomon, David's son had no choice. He had to deal with him; he could not let his actions go unpunished. In consideration of Abiathar's former loyalty to David and his advanced age, Solomon spared the old priest's life, but *banished* him from the capitol (Jerusalem) and sent him to his home to live out his few remaining years.

Solomon's Third Move: Dealing with David's Most Dangerous Enemy

Young King Solomon was forced to do something in his first days as king that his father had been unable to do for forty years! He had to deal with deadly Joab, the battle-hardened schemer who had commanded David's armies for decades.

When old General Joab saw Solomon move quickly and decisively against Prince Adonijah and Abiathar the priest, he knew he was *next*. According to the Bible record, Joab's reaction this time didn't bear any resemblance to his bold and arrogant actions to danger in previous years. This time, the old assassin and military commander ran to the tabernacle of God and took hold of the altar, hoping his repentance in such a holy place would save him.

Joab learned quickly that it was "too little, too late." Solomon had General Benaiah execute Joab on the spot without mercy (see Kings 2:28–34).

(Many people feel erroneously that God's mercy is so great that it will override all of the warnings about God's righteousness and the final judgment in the Bible. Some even go into heresy and say there is no hell and there will be no judgment. I'm concerned that they may feel the same emotions that probably surged through Joab's heart the moment he realized he was about to experience the *unavoidable consequence* of his own choices in life!)

Joab had become little more than a ruthless killer with a lofty job title. He spent his life for himself alone, extending mock loyalty to his uncle David only when it was beneficial to his own cause or desires. His consuming appetite for personal power led him to betray the king who was God's anointed! In the end, Joab the pitiless killer was cut down at the altar of a God whom he had despised and had tried to use for his own purposes.

King Solomon's Final Move:
Dealing with Shimei

Solomon's father, King David, had kept his vow to Shimei that he would not put him to death in his lifetime. But David had passed on, the vow was now void, and Shimei was still a potential threat to the house of David and to his son the king. Here we see the wisdom of God revealed in Solomon's dealings with his father's old enemy (see 1 Kings 2:36–46).

Old Shimei was a skilled survivor as well as a foul-mouthed loyalist to Saul's house. He remembered the vow King David made to him after he met David's entourage as it was returning to Jerusalem after Absalom's defeat and death. He counted on the righteousness and mercy that David (and now Solomon) had shown consistently over the years. What he didn't count on was his own moral and ethical weakness, and that is *exactly* what wise King Solomon counted on.

> And the king sent and called for Shimei, and said unto him, Build thee an house in Jerusalem, and dwell there, and go not forth thence any whither.
>
> For it shall be, that on the day thou goest out, and passest over the brook Kidron, thou shalt know for certain that thou shalt surely die: thy blood shall be upon thine own head.

225

> And Shimei said unto the king, The saying is good: as my lord the king hath said, so will thy servant do (1 Kings 2:36–38).

Solomon knew from his father's experience and his warning that he couldn't trust Shimei's sham loyalty to the throne. However, he *knew* he could trust in the old mocker's presumptive nature and selfish instincts. Royal decree or not, something would come up that would lead that lawless man to dismiss the king's command—and the consequence of his action would indeed "be on his own head."

Shimei managed to keep his agreement and enjoy his royal pardon for three years, but his greedy insistence to personally recover two slaves who had fled to a Philistine city proved to be his undoing. He *could* have hired someone else to pursue the slaves, he *could* have asked a son or some other family member to make the trip, but he must have felt sure the king had forgotten about him.

As soon as King Solomon heard the news, he summoned him and had Shimei summarily *executed* by Benaiah, the new general of Israel's army.

Swiftly and surely, King Solomon secured his throne against the key individuals who had given his father, King David, countless sleepless nights and unwanted anxiety. He was ready now to rule. The mantle had been passed, a new generation had received the legacy, and David could rest in peace.

David's Enduring Legacy with God and Man

When you consider that the Old Testament refers to David's life more than any other, it is surprising that there are so few individual testimonies to him in the Scriptures. In summary, this is what might appear on David's obituary if it were to appear in a newspaper today, based on the written records of his life:

1. David the son of Jesse ruled Judah in Hebron *seven* years.

2. He ruled united Israel in Jerusalem for *thirty-three* years.

3. He died at a *full* age, or in the Authorized terminology, *"full of days."*

4. David ended his life with enormous *wealth*.

5. He enjoyed great *honor* during his final years.

In stark contrast, David has an astounding *divine testimony* consisting of three remarkable tributes given to him by God Himself! It is this trilogy of divine honor that tells the real story of the Sweet Psalmist of Israel. It is almost as if God reserved to Himself the writing of David's obituary!

The Lord did it in three parts in conjunction with three *revelations* of His protection and provision to Solomon, David's chosen successor to his throne.

God's *First* Tribute to David

Solomon's first task when he came to the throne was to pray for wisdom as the new king. According to the Scriptures, God appeared to Solomon in a dream during the night. He said He was pleased with Solomon and promised him not only wisdom but also great wealth and honor *above anyone* who had ever lived before him.

It was then that these words came from the mouth of God Himself as a *promise* to Solomon and as a *divine tribute* to David:

"I will do what you have asked. I will give you a wise and discerning heart, so that there will never have been anyone like you, nor will there ever be. Moreover, I will give you what you have not asked for—both riches and honor— so that in your lifetime you will have no equal among kings. And if you walk in my ways and obey my statutes and commands *as David your father did*, I will give you a long life" (1 Kings 3:12–14, NIV, emphasis mine).

God's *Second* Tribute to David

The *second* divine tribute to David came seven years later when Solomon finished the Temple in Jerusalem and dedicated it to the Lord. That is when God again appeared to Solomon and declared His great esteem for David in these words:

> "As for you, if you walk before me in integrity of heart and uprightness, *as David your father did*, and do all I command and observe my decrees and laws, I will establish your royal throne over Israel forever, as *I promised David your father* when I said, 'You shall never fail to have a man on the throne of Israel'" (1 Kings 9:4–5, NIV, emphasis mine).

This was a divine reaffirmation of the prophetic promise God gave to King David through Nathan the prophet, the very promise that David *"hid in his heart that he might not sin against the Lord"* (2 Samuel 7:16–17).

God's *Third* Tribute to David

God's *third tribute* to David came from the lips of the apostle Paul as he preached his first recorded apostolic sermon in Antioch of Pisidia. Paul's famous words have forever immortalized David in our hearts, and they set a high standard of personal love, intimacy, and faithfulness to God:

> After this, God gave them judges until the time of Samuel the prophet. Then the people asked for a king, and he gave them Saul son of Kish, of the tribe of

Benjamin, who ruled forty years. After removing Saul, he made David their king. *He testified concerning him:* "I have found David son of Jesse *a man after my own heart*; he will do everything I want him to do."

From this man's descendants God has brought to Israel the Savior Jesus, as he promised (Acts 13:20–23, NIV, emphasis mine).

What a tribute! This one-sentence tribute from God naming David as "a man after my own heart" is *unique* in the pages of Scripture. Perhaps you noticed that we included the following verse. We did it because the meaning and value of that verse is even greater!

Think of it this way: What if God were referring to *your* name in this passage? "From *this man's descendants* God has brought to Israel the Savior Jesus, as he promised" (Acts 13:23, NIV, emphasis mine).

David left behind him a legacy that has become a blessing to *all of us!* Imagine the Son of God taking on *your name* during His earthly ministry! What would it be like to know that Jesus would stand before the world and call Himself "the Son of Ron," or "the Son of Karen"? We will never know those things, but we *do know* the impact brought to this planet by the One called "the Son of David"!

It was not David's noble *birth* or his *wealth* that

produced this coveted legacy. David didn't have a noble birth, and he was born into a humble shepherd's home (although Jesse probably was a local chieftain in that rural district of Bethlehem).

There was one thing only that sustained David through all of his difficulties:

- the rejections of his childhood;
- the calamities of his family;
- the fierce wars of his kingdom;
- the crushing failures of his personal life.

That one thing, and the true legacy of this great man passed down to us today is this, summed up perfectly in the words of the apostle Paul:

He was a man after God's own heart.

Isaiah the prophet still cries out to you and to me across the centuries and unfolding human history, "Seek the LORD while he may be found; call on him while he is near" (Isaiah 55:6, NIV).

This was the simple secret that set apart David the shepherd boy from every boy and girl who preceded him, and from everyone born after him. It was the secret of his power, and the sole foundation for his legacy in God—he sought the Lord with all of his heart.

We can all aspire to that! It is possible and available to every one of us through the life, ministry, sacrifice, and resurrection of Jesus Christ. Whether or not you achieve it depends solely upon you.

BIBLIOGRAPHY

Bonhoeffer, D. *Temptation*. New York: MacMillan, 1953.

Keil, C. F. and F. Delitzche. *Commentary on the Old Testament*, vol. 2. Grand Rapids: Eerdmans, 1982.

Keller, W. Phillip. *David, the Shepherd King*, vol. 2. Waco, TX: Word Books, 1996.

Krummacher, F. W. *David, King of Israel*. Trans. M. G. Easton. Grand Rapids: Kregel Classics, 1994. (Originally published by T&T Clark, Edinburgh.)

Meyer, F. B. *David: Shepherd, Psalmist, King*. Fort Washington, PA: Christian Literature Crusade, 1990.

Redpath, Alan. *The Making of a Man of God*. Grand Rapids: Fleming H. Revell, 1962.

Rosenburg, David. *The Book of David*. New York: Harmony Books, 1997.

Swindoll, Charles R. *David, a Man of Passion and Destiny*. Dallas: Word, 1997.

Known as "scholarship on fire," Dr. Cottle's teaching is clear, dynamic and inspirational. His unique style always contains the compassion of a shepherd, the urgency of a prophet and the wisdom of a statesman. His thoughts and counsel are straightforward, dynamic and powerful. Perhaps no modern Bible teacher writes more clearly or convincingly than Ronald Cottle. His teachings will help today's spiritual leaders and other sincere "thinking Christians" to discover the mystery and the majesty of the Bible.

Other Titles by Dr. Cottle Include:

ANOINTED TO REIGN: David's Pathway to Rulership

Fan the flames of your passion for God through Dr. Cottle's insightful study of David's training for the throne of Israel. David's life, his strengths and weaknesses, are laid bare in this book, yet Dr. Cottle still conveys the inescapable sense of God's presence in David's life as God draws him into his special destiny. This sensitive account of David's journey into destiny is designed to help you become all God has designed you to be. (Available in Spanish.)

GALATIANS

This commentary takes you on an expositional journey into the compelling truths of Paul's teachings to the Galatian believers. In this book, you will discover hidden truths and fresh insight into some of the most crucial Pauline teachings in the New Testament. (Available in Spanish.)

THE CROWN PRINCE ANOINTING: Your Mantle of Anointing in this Time of Transition

This book is intended to prepare leaders for the harvest that is just ahead. Dr. Cottle writes: "It is not for the leaders of my generation. We've had our opportunities and, for the most part, allowed them to slip by us; the next generation of leaders will be those who gather in the harvest." (Available in Spanish.)

HOW TO RESPOND TO CRITICISM

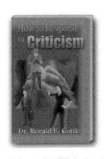

What should you do when you are criticized? How does it make you feel? Is there a right, biblical response? There is a right response, and in this CD book Dr. Ron Cottle tells you how to achieve it. This insightful message has saved marriages, church splits, and parent-child separations. Everyone needs to have this teaching.

HOW TO CONFRONT:
The Art of Godly, Successful Confrontation

Most often we do not practice godly confrontation when someone offends us because of our fear of conflict, ignorance of how to do it lovingly, anger, or embarrassment. There is a right way to confront which will win every time. In this CD book, Dr. Ron Cottle tells you how. It is biblical, loving, spiritual and will bring good results.

Other Books:

Simple Studies on Faith

Harnessing Your Potential

How to Have a Happy Family

Studies in Nehemiah

Ten Commandments

Lectures on Leadership Volume I

Lectures on Leadership Volume II

Other CD Books:

What Do You Do When God Says No?

First Fruits Seed Offering: Realizing God's Abundance Now!

Going to the Next Level

For information about these and many other resources, please visit:
www.roncottleministries.com

Authorized Site and Use License

Definitions

The "Licensed Property" is the *Christian Life School of Theology Global course contents and delivery systems*, hereafter referred to as "Curriculum." The "Owner" of the Curriculum is Christian Life School of Theology Global and is protected by United States and foreign copyright and other intellectual property laws. The "Authorized Site Licensee" is the party or representative of the party entering into this agreement with CLST Global. An "Authorized User" is any staff member of the Licensee, authorized representative, Locally Authorized Teacher, or student using any or all elements of the Licensed Property. The "Site" is the CLEN member school, its programs and students. The "Site" may also be an individual Distance Education student entering into this agreement.

Agreement

Christian Life School of Theology Global hereby grants to the designated Authorized Site Licensee, and the Licensee hereby accepts, a personal, non-exclusive, revocable, non-transferable License to access and use the Curriculum subject to the terms and conditions set forth herein. CLST Global grants to the Licensee and/or all Authorized Users a license to use the Curriculum at the Licensee's Site. All prior agreements, representations, and communications relating to the same subject are superseded by this Agreement. This Agreement may not be modified other than by a written document signed by an authorized representative of each party.

Terms

The Licensed Property may only be used for purposes of education or other non-commercial use. Content will not be used or shared outside of the Licensees' Site. This agreement does not permit anyone other than Authorized Users to use the Curriculum nor permit Authorized Users to use the Curriculum for any uses other than Authorized Uses. Licensee shall not use, or authorize or permit any Student or Staff to use, the Curriculum for any other purpose or in any other manner. The Licensee shall not use the Curriculum for commercial purposes, including but not limited to sale of the Curriculum or bulk reproduction or distribution of the Curriculum, or any portion thereof, in any form. The Licensee may not sell, lend, lease, rent, assign, or transfer the Curriculum to another party in any form. The Licensee may not translate, disassemble, or create derivative works based upon the Curriculum or any part thereof, without the written permission of CLST Global. The Licensee shall make reasonable efforts to prevent Unauthorized Uses of the Licensed Property.

Made in the USA
Middletown, DE
14 September 2020

19623343R00135